THE RARE JEWEL
OF
CHRISTIAN CONTENTMENT

The Rare Jewel
of
Christian Contentment

JEREMIAH BURROUGHS

THE BANNER OF TRUTH TRUST

THE BANNER OF TRUTH TRUST
3 Murrayfield Road, Edinburgh EH12 6EL
P.O. Box 621, Carlisle, Pennsylvania 17013, USA

*

First published 1648
First Banner of Truth Trust edition 1964
Reprinted 1979
Reprinted 1987
Reprinted 1992
Reprinted 1995
Reprinted 1998
ISBN 0 85151 091 4

*

*

Printed and bound in Finland by WSOY

CONTENTS

JEREMIAH BURROUGHS combined harmoniously in his own person what might be considered incompatible qualities: a fervent zeal for purity of doctrine and worship, and a peaceable spirit, which longed and laboured for Christian unity. For the first of these qualities the Puritans are renowned; in the second, they are deemed by some critics to have been deficient. A close study of the problem suggests that, as a whole, the Puritans were no more and no less concerned about the visible unity of the Church than is the Word of God. But in the case of Burroughs, certainly, we are faced with a man who, among his contemporaries and colleagues, was recognized as outstanding for his conciliatory temper and efforts.

The often-quoted opinion of Richard Baxter was that if all the Episcopalians had been like Archbishop Ussher, all the Presbyterians like Stephen Marshall, and all the Independents like Jeremiah Burroughs, then the breaches of the Church would soon have been healed. Of Burroughs himself, it was said that his heart was broken by the divisions among the Puritan reformers in the 1640's and that this contributed to his premature death at the age of forty-seven.

The life and ministry of Burroughs, though comparatively short, exemplify many of the best features of the era to which he belonged. Born in 1599, he was educated at Emmanuel College, Cambridge. Founded in 1584 on the site of an old Dominican college, Emmanuel became the greatest seminary of Puritan preachers. Through it passed Thomas Hooker, John Cotton, Thomas Shepard (all of them founding fathers in New England), as well as Stephen Marshall, William Bridge, Anthony Burgess, Thomas Brooks and Thomas Watson. It is recorded that, while still at Cambridge, Burroughs was a nonconformist and eventually he was forced to leave the university for this reason.

Jeremiah Burroughs' ministry falls readily into three periods: 1. After leaving Cambridge, he ministered to two congregations in East Anglia, the region where the influence of Puritan principles was strongest. This ended in 1636 when he was suspended, and then deprived. 2. In 1637 he responded to a call to serve the English Church at Rotterdam, where he stayed for four years. 3. The final period, up to his death in 1646, witnessed his greatest success as a popular preacher in London and a leading reformer of the Independent persuasion.

1. In his first charge, at Bury St Edmunds, Burroughs' colleague was Edmund Calamy, who was also later to be a famous city preacher, as well as a leading writer (one of the co-authors of the tract *Smectymnuus* against the episcopacy and liturgy of the Church of England) and a church leader (after the Restoration of Charles II, he refused a bishopric). In 1631 Burroughs was appointed Rector of Tivetshall, Norfolk. Although East Anglia was a Puritan stronghold, his position was soon in jeopardy as the bishops, under the over-all direction of Laud, were determined to enforce nation-wide conformity. Bishop Wren of Norwich (later of Ely) was one of the most severe and bigoted members of the episcopal bench. By means of his visitation articles, he insisted on the placing of the communion table altarwise, encouraged superstitious gestures (not countenanced by the Prayer Book) and prohibited afternoon sermons on the Lord's day, as well as requiring all ministers to read the 'Book of Sports', which urged the people to engage in various recreations on the Lord's day after attending morning worship. Several godly ministers were suspended by Wren for nonconformity or for refusing to read the 'Book of Sports', among them Calamy, Bridge and Burroughs himself.

2. The Laudian régime caused not only Puritan ministers but many citizens and church members to leave England, seeking liberty to worship God according to Scripture and their consciences. Some crossed the Atlantic to found a New England. Others, like the Protestant Reformers a century before, sought haven on the Continent. In the 1630's Holland, which had shaken off the yoke of Roman Catholic Spain, was especially hospitable to the exiles. A succession of noted divines ministered to the English congregations there. The learned Dr William Ames, formerly Professor of Theology at the University of Franeker, became teacher of the English Church at Rotterdam in 1632 (though he died the next year), and Burroughs agreed in 1637 to fulfil the same office. His course continued to run parallel to that of William Bridge who, after being forced to leave his charge at Norwich by Bishop Wren, joined Burroughs at Rotterdam as Pastor of the Church. (The Independents, like the New England Congregationalists, regarded the offices of pastor and teacher as distinct, though of course similar.)

3. The Long Parliament, which ended many of the objectionable features of the Laudian era, invited the exiled ministers, among them Burroughs, to return to England. He came back in 1642 to play an important dual role, as a city preacher and as one of the framers of the new religious settlement. In the latter capacity, he was summoned to take his place as a member of the Westminster Assembly. Burroughs played a full part in the work of the Assembly, though he was among the small group of Independents who opposed certain features of the form of church government agreed to by the majority of the Assembly. The 'Five Dissenting Brethren', as the Independent leaders were called, were, however, in full doctrinal agreement with the other Puritans, and Burroughs, especially, deplored the deep division which ensued. One of his most famous works was *Irenicum* or *Heart-Divisions Opened*, in which he pleaded for the unity of all who loved the truth, and argued that what made comparatively minor differences into causes of rigid divisions was a wrong spirit and wrong motives.

His efforts to promote a united church settlement were to prove unsuccessful, though many of the leading Puritan ministers kept, like him, a true sense of proportion.

In the period of Parliament's ascendancy, many of the ablest preachers gravitated towards London, and Burroughs was chosen to preach at Stepney and Cripplegate, described on the title-page of the first edition of *The Rare Jewel of Christian Contentment* as 'two of the greatest congregations in England'. At Stepney he shared the ministry with William Greenhill, famous for his Commentary on Ezekiel, so that Burroughs (who preached at 7 a.m.) was called the morning-star of Stepney, and Greenhill the evening-star.

The substance of Burroughs' preaching is revealed in his published works, which are mainly sermons. These writings, most of which were published posthumously, were extremely popular in the seventeenth century, but they have never been collected and issued as a complete set. It is rather surprising that, in the last century, when the works of many Puritan divines were re-published, only two of Burroughs' were chosen, his *Exposition of Hosea* and *Sermons on the Beatitudes*.[1] This, at any rate, is not commensurate with the high esteem in which he was held by his fellow-Puritans.

Perhaps one difficulty for modern readers in Burroughs' works is the very homeliness which must have commended them to his own generation. Consequently, in the present reprint, an attempt has been made, here and there, to render the work more intelligible to modern readers by means of slight modification of language and punctuation. No apology is needed for Burroughs' substance, which remains unchanged. His grasp of doctrine, discernment into the very recesses of the human heart, comprehensive and profound knowledge of Scripture and ability to apply it, and superb gift of illustration, are all exemplified in this book.

The Rare Jewel was first published in 1648, two years after

[1] These two works were issued in the famous series of reprints by James Nichol of Edinburgh. Our attention has been drawn by Mr S. M. Houghton of Oxford to a series entitled 'The Young Christian's Pocket Library', published in six volumes in 1836 by Fisher and Jackson of London, in which *The Rare Jewel of Christian Contentment* is printed in its entirety.

the author's premature death. It was prefaced, and presumably sponsored, by several eminent divines including Bridge, Greenhill, Thomas Goodwin, Philip Nye and Sidrach Simpson. They conclude their preface as this biographical note may appropriately conclude by pointing to the author's object in writing: 'The only seat this (Jewel of Contentment) is ordained for is the precious tablets of men's hearts, in and from which alone the native lustre of it will be made conspicuous. Reader, buy it, set and wear it there, and it shall, as Solomon speaks, "be life unto thy soul, and grace unto thy neck. Thou shalt not be afraid when thou liest down; yea, thy sleep shall be sweet unto thee: for the Lord will be thy confidence".'

MICHAEL BOLAND

September, 1964

I

CHRISTIAN CONTENTMENT DESCRIBED

—————

*'I have learned, in whatsoever state I am, therewith
to be content'* (Philippians 4. 11)

This text contains a very timely cordial to revive the drooping
spirits of the saints in these sad and sinking times. For the
'hour of temptation' has already come upon all the world to
try the inhabitants of the earth. In particular, this is the day of
Jacob's trouble in our own bowels.

Our great Apostle holds forth experimentally in this Gospel-
text the very life and soul of all practical divinity. In it we may
plainly read his own proficiency in the school of Christ, and
what lesson every Christian who would prove the power and
growth of godliness in his own soul must necessarily learn
from him.

These words are brought in by Paul as a clear argument to
persuade the Philippians that he did not seek after great things
in the world, and that he sought not 'theirs' but 'them'. He
did not long for great wealth. His heart was taken up with
better things. 'I do not speak', he says, 'in respect of want, for
whether I have or have not, my heart is fully satisfied, I have
enough: I have learned in whatsoever state I am, therewith to
be content.'

'I have learned' – Contentment in every condition is a great
art, a spiritual mystery. It is to be learned, and to be learned
as a mystery. And so in verse 12 he affirms: 'I know how to be
abased, and I know how to abound: everywhere and in all

[17]

things I am instructed.' The word which is translated 'instructed' is derived from the word that signifies 'mystery'; it is just as if he had said, 'I have learned the mystery of this business.' Contentment is to be learned as a great mystery, and those who are thoroughly trained in this art, which is like Samson's riddle to a natural man, have learned a deep mystery. 'I have learned it' – I do not have to learn it now, nor did I have the art at first; I have attained it, though with much ado, and now, by the grace of God, I have become the master of this art.

'In whatsoever state I am' – The word 'estate' is not in the original, but simply 'in what I am', that is, in whatever concerns or befalls me, whether I have little or nothing at all.

'Therewith to be content' – The word rendered 'content' here has great elegance and fulness of meaning in the original. In the strict sense it is only attributed to God, who has styled himself 'God all-sufficient', in that he rests fully satisfied in and with himself alone. But he is pleased freely to communicate his fulness to the creature, so that from God in Christ the saints receive 'grace for grace' (John 1. 16). As a result, there is in them the same grace that is in Christ, according to their measure. In this sense, Paul says, I have a *self-sufficiency*, which is what the word means.

But has Paul got a self-sufficiency? you will say. How are we sufficient of ourselves? Our Apostle affirms in another case, 'That we are not sufficient of ourselves to think anything as of ourselves' (2 Corinthians 3. 5). Therefore his meaning must be, I find a sufficiency of satisfaction in my own heart, through the grace of Christ that is in me. Though I have not outward comforts and worldly conveniences to supply my necessities, yet I have a sufficient portion between Christ and my soul abundantly to satisfy me in every condition. This interpretation agrees with that place: 'A good man is satisfied from himself' (Proverbs 14. 14) and also with what Paul avers of himself in another place, that 'though he had nothing yet he possessed all things'. Because he had a right to the covenant and promise, which virtually contains everything, and an interest in Christ, the fountain and good of all, it is no marvel that he said that in whatsoever state he was in, he was content.

Thus you have the true interpretation of the text. I shall not make any division of the words, because I take them only to promote that one most necessary duty, viz. quieting and comforting the hearts of God's people under the troubles and changes they meet with in these heart-shaking times. The doctrinal conclusion briefly is this: *That to be well skilled in the mystery of Christian contentment is the duty, glory and excellence of a Christian.*

This evangelical truth is held forth sufficiently in the Scripture, yet we may take one or two more parallel places to confirm it. In 1 Timothy 6. 6 and 8 you find expressed both the duty and the glory of it: 'Having food and raiment', he says in verse 8, 'let us be therewith content' – there is the duty. 'But godliness with contentment is great gain' (v. 6) – there is the glory and excellence of it; as if to suggest that godliness were not gain except contentment be with it. The same exhortation you have in Hebrews: 'Let your conversation be without covetousness, and be content with such things as you have' (Hebrews 13. 5). I do not find any Apostle or writer of Scripture who deals so much with this spiritual mystery of contentment as this our Apostle has done throughout his Epistles.

To explain and prove the above conclusion, I shall endeavour to demonstrate four things:

1. The nature of this Christian contentment: what it is.
2. The art and mystery of it.
3. What lessons must be learned to bring the heart to contentment.
4. Wherein the glorious excellence of this grace chiefly consists.

I offer the following description: *Christian contentment is that sweet, inward, quiet, gracious frame of spirit, which freely submits to and delights in God's wise and fatherly disposal in every condition.*

I shall break open this description, for it is a box of precious ointment, and very comforting and useful for troubled hearts, in troubled times and conditions.

1. Contentment is a sweet, *inward* heart-thing. It is a work of the Spirit indoors.

It is not only that we do not seek to help ourselves by outward violence, or that we forbear from discontented and murmuring expressions with perverse words and bearing against God and others. But it is the inward submission of the heart. 'Truly, my soul waiteth upon God' (Psalm 62. 1) and 'My soul, wait thou only upon God' (verse 5) – so it is in your Bibles, but the words may be translated as correctly: 'My soul, be thou silent unto God. Hold thy peace, O my soul.' Not only must the tongue hold its peace; the soul must be silent. Many may sit silently, refraining from discontented expressions, yet inwardly they are bursting with discontent. This shows a complicated disorder and great perversity in their hearts. And notwithstanding their outward silence, God hears the peevish, fretful language of their souls. A shoe may be smooth and neat outside, while inside it pinches the flesh. Outwardly there may be great calmness and stillness, yet within amazing confusion, bitterness, disturbance and vexation.

Some people are so weak that they cannot restrain the unrest of their spirits, but in words and behaviour they reveal what woeful disturbances there are within. Their spirits are like the raging sea, casting forth nothing but mire and dirt, and are troublesome not only to themselves but also to all with whom they live. Others, however, are able to restrain such disorders of heart, as Judas did when he betrayed Christ with a kiss, but even so they boil inwardly and eat away like a canker. So David speaks of some whose words are sweeter than honey and butter, and yet have war in their hearts. In another place, he says, 'While I kept silence my bones waxed old'. In the same way these people, while there is a serene calm upon their tongues, have blustering storms upon their spirits, and while they keep silence their hearts are troubled and even worn away with anguish and vexation. They have

[20]

peace and quiet outwardly, but within war from the unruly and turbulent workings of their hearts.

If the attainment of true contentment were as easy as keeping quiet outwardly, it would not need much learning. It might be had with less strength and skill than an Apostle possessed, yea, less than an ordinary Christian has or may have. Therefore, there is certainly more to it than can be attained by common gifts and the ordinary power of reason, which often bridle nature. It is a business of the heart.

II. It is the *quiet* of the heart. All is sedate and still there. That you may understand this better, I would add that this quiet, gracious frame of spirit is not opposed to certain things :

1. *To a due sense of affliction.* God gives his people leave to be sensible of what they suffer. Christ does not say, 'Do not count as a cross what is a cross'; he says, 'Take up your cross daily'. It is like physical health : if you take medicine and cannot hold it, but immediately vomit it up, or if you feel nothing and it does not move you – in either case the medicine does no good, but suggests that you are greatly disordered and will hardly be cured. So it is with the spirits of men under afflictions : if they cannot bear God's potions and bring them up again, or if they are insensitive to them and no more affected by them than the body is by a draught of small beer, it is a sad symptom that their souls are in a dangerous and almost incurable condition. So this inward quietness is not in opposition to a sense of afflictions, for, indeed, there would be no true contentment if you were not apprehensive and sensible of your afflictions, when God is angry.

2. *It is not opposed to making in an orderly manner our moan and complaint to God, and to our friends.* Though a Christian ought to be quiet under God's correcting hand, he may without any breach of Christian contentment complain to God. As one of the ancients says, Though not with a tumultuous clamour and shrieking out in a confused passion, yet in a quiet, still, submissive way he may unbosom his heart to God. Likewise he may communicate his sad condition to his Christian friends, showing them how God has dealt with him,

and how heavy the affliction is upon him, that they may speak a word in season to his weary soul.

3. *It is not opposed to all lawful seeking for help in different circumstances, nor to endeavouring simply to be delivered out of present afflictions by the use of lawful means.* No, I may lay in provision for my deliverance and use God's means, waiting on him because I do not know but that it may be his will to alter my condition. And so far as he leads me I may follow his providence; it is but my duty. God is thus far mercifully indulgent to our weakness, and he will not take it ill at our hands if by earnest and importunate prayer we seek him for deliverance until we know his good pleasure in the matter. Certainly seeking thus for help, with such submission and holy resignation of spirit, to be delivered when God wills, and as God wills, and how God wills, so that our wills are melted into the will of God – this is not opposed to the quietness which God requires in a contented spirit.

But what, then, it will be asked, *is* this quietness of spirit opposed to?

1. *It is opposed to murmuring and repining at the hand of God,* as the discontented Israelites often did. If we cannot bear this either in our children or servants, much less can God bear it in us.

2. *To vexing and fretting,* which is a degree beyond murmuring. I remember the saying of a heathen, 'A wise man may grieve for, but not be vexed with his afflictions'. There is a vast difference between a kindly grieving and a disordered vexation.

3. *To tumultuousness of spirit,* when the thoughts run distractingly and work in a confused manner, so that the affections are like the unruly multitude in the Acts, who did not know for what purpose they had come together. The Lord expects you to be silent under his rod, and, as was said in Acts 19. 36, 'Ye ought to be quiet and to do nothing rashly.'

4. *It is opposed to an unsettled and unstable spirit, whereby the heart is distracted from the present duty that God requires in our several relationships, towards God, ourselves and others.*

[22]

We should prize duty more highly than to be distracted by every trivial occasion. Indeed, a Christian values every service of God so much that though some may be in the eyes of the world and of natural reason a slight and empty business, beggarly elements, or foolishness, yet since God calls for it, the authority of the command so overawes his heart that he is willing to spend himself and to be spent in discharging it. It is an expression of Luther's that ordinary works, done in faith and from faith, are more precious than heaven and earth. And if this is so, and a Christian knows it, he should not be diverted by small matters, but should answer every distraction, and resist every temptation, as Nehemiah did Sanballat, Geshem and Tobiah, when they would have hindered the building of the wall, with this : 'I am doing a great work so that I cannot come down : why should the work cease, whilst I leave it, and come down to you?' (Nehemiah 6. 3).

5. *It is opposed to distracting, heart-consuming cares.* A gracious heart so esteems its union with Christ and the work that God sets it about that it will not willingly suffer anything to come in to choke it or deaden it. A Christian is desirous that the Word of God should take such full possession as to divide between soul and spirit (Hebrews 4. 12), but he would not allow the fear and noise of evil tidings to take such a hold in his soul as to make a division and struggling there, like the twins in Rebekah's womb. A great man will permit common people to stand outside his doors, but he will not let them come in and make a noise in his closet or bedroom when he deliberately retires from all worldly business. So a well-tempered spirit may enquire after things outside in the world, and suffer some ordinary cares and fears to break into the suburbs of the soul, so as to touch lightly upon the thoughts. Yet it will not on any account allow an intrusion into the private room, which should be wholly reserved for Jesus Christ as his inward temple.

6. *It is opposed to sinking discouragements.* When things do not fall out according to expectation, when the tide of second causes runs so low that we see little in outward means to sup-

port our hopes and hearts, then the heart begins to reason as did he in 2 Kings 7. 2 : 'If the Lord should open the windows of heaven how should this be?' We never consider that God can open the eyes of the blind with clay and spittle, he can work above, beyond, and even contrary to means. He often makes the fairest flowers of man's endeavours to wither and brings improbable things to pass, in order that the glory of the undertaking may be given to himself. Indeed, if his people stand in need of miracles to bring about their deliverance, miracles fall as easily from God's hands as to give his people daily bread. God's blessing many times is a secret from his servants so that they do not know from which way it is coming, as 'Ye shall not see wind, neither shall ye see rain, yet the valley shall be filled with water' (2 Kings 3. 17). God would have us to depend on him though we do not see how the thing may be brought about; otherwise we do not show a quiet spirit. Though an affliction is on you, do not let your heart sink under it. So far as your heart sinks and you are discouraged under affliction, so much you need to learn this lesson of contentment.

7. *It is opposed to sinful shiftings and shirkings to get relief and help.* We see this kind of thing in Saul running to the witch of Endor, and offering sacrifice before Samuel came. Nay, good King Jehoshaphat joins himself with Ahaziah (2 Chronicles 20. 35). And Asa goes to Benhadad, King of Syria, for help, 'not relying upon the Lord' (2 Chronicles 16. 7, 8), though the Lord had delivered the Ethiopian army into his hands consisting of a thousand thousand (2 Chronicles 14. 12). And good Jacob joined with his mother in lying to Isaac; not content to await God's time and use God's means, he made too great a haste and went out of his way to procure the blessing which God intended for him. Thus do many, through the corruption of their hearts and the weakness of their faith, because they are not able to trust God and follow him fully in all things and always. For this reason, the Lord often follows the saints with many sore temporal crosses, as we see in the case of Jacob, though they obtain the mercy. It may be that your carnal heart thinks, I do not care how I am delivered, if only I

may be freed from it. Is it not so many times in some of your hearts, when any cross or affliction befalls you? Do you not experience such workings of spirit as this? 'Oh, if I could only be delivered from this affliction in any way, I would not care' –your hearts are far from being quiet. This sinful shifting is the next thing which is in opposition to the quietness which God requires in a contented spirit.

8. The last thing that quietness of spirit is the opposite of is *desperate risings of the heart against God by way of rebellion.* That is the most abominable. I hope many of you have learned so far to be content as to restrain your hearts from such disorders. Yet the truth is that not only wicked men, but sometimes the very saints of God find the beginnings of this, when an affliction remains for a long time and is very severe and heavy indeed upon them, and strikes them, as it were, in the master vein. They find in their hearts something of a rising against God, their thoughts begin to bubble, and their affections begin to move in rebellion against God himself. Especially is this the case with those who besides their corruptions have a large measure of melancholy. The Devil works both upon the corruptions of their hearts and the melancholy disease of their bodies, and though much grace may lie underneath, yet under affliction there may be some risings against God himself.

Now Christian quietness is opposed to all these things. When affliction comes, whatever it is, you do not murmur; though you feel it, though you make your cry to God, though you desire to be delivered, and seek it by all good means, yet you do not murmur or repine, you do not fret or vex yourself, there is not a tumultuousness of spirit in you, not an instability, there are not distracting fears in your hearts, no sinking discouragements, no unworthy shifts, no risings in rebellion against God in any way: This is quietness of spirit under an affliction, and that is the second thing, when the soul is so far able to bear an affliction as to keep quiet under it.

III. Now the next thing I want to explain in the description is this, It is an inward, quiet, gracious *frame* of spirit. It is a frame of spirit and also a gracious frame. Contentment is a soul business. First, it is inward; Secondly, quiet; Thirdly, it is a quiet *frame* of spirit. I mean three things when I say that contentment consists in the quiet *frame* of the spirit of a man.

1. *That it is a grace that spreads itself through the whole soul.* It is in the judgment, that is, the judgment of the soul of a man or woman tends to quiet the heart – in my judgment I am satisfied. It is one thing to be satisfied in one's judgment and understanding, so as to be able to say, 'This is the hand of God, and is what is suitable to my condition or best for me. Although I do not see the reason for the thing, yet I am satisfied in my judgment about it.' Then it is in the thoughts of a man or woman. As my judgment is satisfied, so my thoughts are kept in order. And then it comes to the will. My will yields and submits to it; my affections are likewise kept in order, so that it goes through the whole soul.

In some there is a partial contentment. It is not the frame of the soul, but some part of the soul has some contentment. Many a man may be satisfied in his judgment about a thing who cannot for his life rule his affections, nor his thoughts, nor his will. I do not doubt that many of you know this in your own experience, if you observe the workings of your own hearts. Can you not say when a certain affliction befalls you, I can bless God that I am satisfied in my judgment about it; I have nothing to say about it in respect of my judgment about it? I see the hand of God and I should be content, yea, in my judgment I am satisfied that mine is a good condition. But I cannot for my life rule my thoughts and will and my affections. Methinks I feel my heart heavy and sad and more than it should be; yet my judgment is satisfied. This seemed to be the position of David in Psalm 42 : 'O my soul, why art thou disquieted?' As far as David's judgment went there was a contentedness, that is, his judgment was satisfied as to the work of God on him. He was troubled, but he knew not why : 'O my soul, why art thou cast down within me?'

This is a very good psalm for those who feel a fretting, discontented sickness in their hearts at any time to read and sing. He says once or twice in that Psalm : 'Why art thou cast down, O my soul?' and in verse 5, 'And why art thou disquieted within me? hope thou in God, for I shall yet praise him for the help of his countenance.' David had enough to quiet him, and what he had, prevailed with his judgment. But after it had prevailed with his judgment, he could not get it any further. He could not get this grace of contentment to go through the whole frame of his soul.

Sometimes, a great deal of disturbance is involved in getting contentment into people's judgments, that is, to satisfy their judgment about their condition. If you come to many, whom the hand of God is upon perhaps in a grievous manner, and seek to satisfy them and tell them they have no cause to be so disquieted, 'Oh, no cause?' says the troubled spirit, 'then there is no cause for anyone to be disquieted. There has never been such an affliction as I have.' And they have a hundred things with which to evade the force of what is said to them, so that you cannot so much as get at their judgments to satisfy them. But there is a great deal of hope of attaining contentment, if once your judgments are satisfied, if you can sit down and say in your judgment, 'I see good reason to be contented.' Yet even when you have got so far, you may still have much to do with your hearts afterwards. There is such unruliness in our thoughts and affections that our judgments are not always able to rule our thoughts and affections. That is what makes me say that contentment is an inward, quiet, gracious frame of spirit – the whole soul, judgment, thoughts, will, affections and all are satisfied and quiet. I suppose that merely in opening this subject you begin to see that it is a lesson that you need to learn, and that if contentment is like this then it is not easily obtained.

2. *Spiritual contentment comes from the frame of the soul.* The contentment of a man or woman who is rightly content does not come so much from outward arguments or from any outward help, as from the disposition of their own hearts. The disposition of their own hearts causes and brings forth this gracious contentment rather than any external thing.

Let me explain myself. Someone is disturbed, suppose it to

be a child or a man or a woman. If you come and bring some great thing to please them, perhaps it will quiet them and they will be contented. It is the thing you bring that quiets them, not the disposition of their own spirits, not any good temper in their own hearts, but the external thing you bring them. But when a Christian is content in the right way, the quiet comes more from the temper and disposition of his own heart than from any external argument or from the possession of anything in the world.

I would unfold this further to you with this simile: To be content as a result of some external thing is like warming a man's clothes by the fire. But to be content through an inward disposition of the soul is like the warmth that a man's clothes have from the natural heat of his body. A man who is healthy in body puts on his clothes, and perhaps at first on a cold morning they feel cold. But after he has had them on a little while they are warm. Now, how did they get warm? They were not near the fire? No, this came from the natural heat of his body. Now when a sickly man, the natural heat of whose body has deteriorated, puts on his clothes, they do not get hot after a long time. He must warm them by the fire, and even then they will soon be cold again.

This will illustrate the different contentments of men. Some are very gracious, and when an affliction comes on them, though at first it seems a little cold, after they have borne it a while, the very temper of their hearts makes their afflictions easy. They are quiet under it and do not complain of any discontent. But now there are others that have an affliction upon them and have not this good temper in their hearts. Their afflictions are very cold and troublesome to them. Maybe, if you bring some external arguments to bear upon them like the fire that warms the clothes, they will be quiet for a while. But, alas, if they lack a gracious disposition in their own hearts, that warmth will not last long. The warmth of the fire, that is, a contentment that results merely from external arguments, will not last long. But that which comes from the gracious temper of one's spirit will last. When it comes from the spirit

[28]

of a man or woman – that is true contentment. We shall, however, have more to say of this in explaining the mystery of contentment.

3. *It is the frame of spirit that shows the habitual character of this grace of contentment.* Contentment is not merely one act, just a flash in a good mood. You find many men and women who, if they are in a good mood, will be very quiet. But this will not hold. It is not a constant course. It is not the constant tenor of their spirits to be holy and gracious under affliction. Now I say that contentment is a quiet frame of spirit and by that I mean that you should find men and women in a good mood not only at this or that time, but as the constant tenor and temper of their hearts. A Christian who, in the constant tenor and temper of his heart, can carry himself quietly with constancy has learned this lesson of contentment. Otherwise his Christianity is worth nothing, for no one, however furious in his discontent, will not be quiet when he is in a good mood.

So first, contentment is a heart-business; secondly, it is the quiet of the heart; and then thirdly, it is the frame of the heart.

IV. Contentment is the *gracious* frame of the heart. Indeed, in contentment there is a compound of all graces, if the contentment is spiritual, if it is truly Christian. There is, I say, a compound of all spiritual graces. As in some oils there is a compound of a great many precious ingredients, so it is in this grace of contentment, which we shall say more of in unfolding its excellence. But now the *gracious* frame of spirit is in opposition to three things:

1. *In opposition to the natural quietness of many men and women.* Some are so constituted by nature that they are more still and quiet; others are of a violent and hot constitution and they are more impatient.

2. *In opposition to a sturdy resolution.* Some men through the strength of a sturdy resolution do not seem to be troubled, come what may. So they are not disquieted as much as others.

3. *By way of distinction from the strength of natural*

(*though unsanctified*) *reason, which may quiet the heart in some degree.* But now I say that a gracious frame of spirit is not merely a stillness of the body which comes from its natural constitution and temper, nor a sturdy resolution, nor merely through the strength of reason.

You will ask, In what way is the grace of contentment distinguished from all these? More will be spoken of this when we come to show the mystery of contentment and the lessons to be learned. But now we may speak a little by way of distinction from the natural quietness of men's spirits. Many men and women have such a natural quietness of spirit and such a bodily constitution that you seldom find them disquieted. Now, mark these people and you will see that they are likewise of a very dull spirit in any good matter; they have no quickness nor liveliness of spirit in such matters either. But where contentment of heart springs from grace, the heart is very quick and lively in the service of God. Yea, the more any gracious heart can bring itself to be in a contented disposition, the more fit it is for any service of God. It is very active and lively, not dull, in the service of God. And just as a contented heart is very active and busy in the work of God, so he is very active and busy in sanctifying God's name in the affliction that befalls him.

The difference is very clear: The one whose disposition is quiet is not disquieted as others are, but neither does he show any activeness of spirit to sanctify the name of God in his affliction. But, on the other hand, he whose contentment is of grace is not disquieted and keeps his heart quiet with regard to vexation and trouble, and at the same time is not dull or heavy but very active to sanctify God's name in the affliction that he is experiencing. For if a man is to be free from discontent and worry it is not enough merely not to murmur but you must be active in sanctifying God's name in the affliction. Indeed, this will distinguish it from a sturdy resolution not to be troubled. Though you have a sturdy resolution that you will not be troubled, do you make it a matter of conscience to sanctify God's name in your affliction and is this where your resolution comes from? That is the main thing that brings quietness of heart and helps against discontent in a gracious heart. I say, the desire and care your soul has to sanctify God's name in an affliction is what quietens the soul, and this is what others lack. A quietness which comes from reason only does not do this either. It is said of Socrates that, though he were only a heathen, he would never so much as change his countenance whatever befell him, and he got this power over his spirit merely by the strength of reason and morality. But gracious contentment comes from principles beyond the strength of reason. I cannot develop that until we come to unfold the mystery of spiritual contentment.

I will give you just one mark of the difference between a man or woman who is content in a natural way and one who is content in a spiritual way: Those who are content in a natural way overcome themselves when outward afflictions befall them and are content. They are just as content when they commit sin against God. When they have outward crosses or when God is dishonoured, it is all one to them; whether they themselves are crossed or whether God is crossed. But a gracious heart that is contented with its own affliction, will rise up strongly when God is dishonoured.

V. The fifth characteristic of contentment is *freely* submitting to and taking pleasure in God's disposal. It is a free work of the spirit. There are four things to be explained in this freedom of the spirit:

1. *That the heart is readily brought over.* When someone does a thing freely, he does not need a lot of moving to get him to do it. Many men and women, when afflictions are heavy upon them, may be brought to a state of contentment with great ado. At last, perhaps, they may be brought to quiet their hearts in their affliction, but only with a great deal of trouble, and not at all freely. If I desire a thing of someone else and I get it with much ado and a great deal of trouble, there is no freedom of spirit here. When a man is free in a thing, only mention it and immediately he does it. So if you have learned this art of contentment you will not only be

content and quiet your hearts after a great ado, but as soon as you come to see that it is the hand of God your heart acts readily and closes at once.

2. *It is freely, that is, not by constraint.* Not, as we say, patience by force. Thus many will say that you must be content: 'This is the hand of God and you cannot help it'. Oh, but this is too low an expression for Christians. Yet when Christians come to visit one another, they say, 'Friend (or neighbour), you must be content.' *Must* be content is too low for a Christian. No, it should be, 'Readily and freely I will be content.' It is suitable to my heart to yield to God and to be content. I find it a thing that comes naturally that my soul should be content. Oh, you should answer your friends so who come and tell you that you *must* be content: No, I am *willing* to yield to God, and I am *freely* content. That is the second point about freedom of spirit. Now a free act comes in a rational manner. That is freedom; it does not come through ignorance, because I know of no better condition or because I do not know what my affliction is, but it comes through a sanctified judgment. That is why no creature but a rational creature can do an act of freedom. Liberty of action is only in rational creatures and comes from hence, for that is only freedom that is done in a rational way. Natural freedom is when I, by my judgment, see what is to be done, understand the thing, and my judgment agrees with what I understand: that is done freely. But if a man does something, not understanding what he is doing, he cannot be said to do it freely. Suppose a child was born in prison and never went outside of it. He is content, but why? Because he never knew anything better. His being content is not a free act. But for men and women who know better, who know that the condition they are in is an afflicted and sad condition, and still by a sanctified judgment can bring their hearts to contentment – this is freedom.

3. *This freedom is in opposition to mere stupidity.* A man or woman may be contented merely from lack of sense. This is not free, any more than a man who is paralysed in a deadly way and does not feel it when you nip him is patient freely.

But if someone should have their flesh pinched and feel it, and yet for all that can control themselves and do it freely, that is another matter. So it is here: many are contented out of mere stupidity. They have a dead paralysis upon them. But a gracious heart has sense enough, and yet is contented, and therefore is free.

VI. Contentment is freely *submitting to* and taking pleasure in God's disposal. Submitting to God's disposal — What is that? The word *submit* signifies nothing else but 'to send under'. Thus in one who is discontented the heart will be unruly, and would even get above God so far as discontent prevails. But now comes the grace of contentment and sends it under, for to submit is to send under a thing. Now when the soul comes to see its own unruliness — Is the hand of God bringing an affliction and yet my heart is troubled and discontented — What, it says, will you be above God? Is this not God's hand and must your will be regarded more than God's? O under, under! get you under, O soul! Keep under! keep low! keep under God's feet! You are under God's feet, and keep under his feet! Keep under the authority of God, the majesty of God, the sovereignty of God, the power that God has over you! To keep under, that is to submit. The soul can submit to God at the time when it can send itself under the power and authority and sovereignty and dominion that God has over it. That is the sixth point, but even that is not enough. You have not attained this grace of contentment unless the next point is true of you.

VII. Contentment is *taking pleasure* in God's disposal. This is so when I am well pleased in what God does, in so far as I can see God in it, though, as I said, I may be sensible of the affliction, and may desire that God in his due time would remove it, and may use means to remove it. Yet I am well pleased in so far as God's hand is in it. To be well pleased with God's hand is a higher degree than the previous one. It comes from this: not only do I see that I should be content in this affliction, but I see that there is good in it. I find there is honey in this rock, and so I do not only say, I *must*, or I *will* submit to

God's hand. No, the hand of God is *good*, 'it is good that I am afflicted'. To acknowledge that it is just that I am afflicted is possible in one who is not truly contented. I may be convinced that God deals justly in this matter, he is righteous and just and it is right that I should submit to what he has done; O the Lord has done righteously in all ways! But that is not enough! You must say, 'Good is the hand of the Lord.' It was the expression of old Eli: 'Good is the word of the Lord', when it was a sore and hard word. It was a word that threatened very grievous things to Eli and his house, and yet Eli says, 'Good is the word of the Lord.' Perhaps, some of you may say, like David, 'It is good that I was afflicted', but you must come to this, 'It is good that I *am* afflicted.' Not just good when you see the good fruit it has wrought, but to say when you are afflicted, 'It is good that I am afflicted. Whatever the affliction, yet through the mercy of God mine is a good condition.' It is, indeed, the top and the height of this art of contentment to come to this pitch and to be able to say, 'Well, my condition and afflictions are so and so, and very grievous and sore; yet, through God's mercy, I am in a good condition, and the hand of God is good upon me notwithstanding.'

I should have given you several Scriptures about this, but I will give you one or two, which are very striking. You will think it is a hard lesson to come so far as not only to be quiet but to take pleasure in affliction. 'In the house of the righteous is much treasure, but in the revenues of the wicked is trouble' (Proverbs 15. 6): here is a Scripture to show that a gracious heart has cause to say that it is in a good condition, whatever it is. In the house of the righteous is much treasure; his house – what house? It may be a poor cottage, and perhaps he has scarcely a stool to sit on. Perhaps he is forced to sit on a stump of wood or part of a block instead of a stool, or perhaps he has scarcely a bed to lie on, or a dish to eat in. Yet the Holy Ghost says, 'In the house of the righteous is much treasure.' Let the righteous man be the poorest man in the world – it may be that someone has come and taken all the goods from out of his house for debt. Perhaps his house is plundered and all is gone;

yet still, 'In the house of the righteous is much treasure.' The righteous man can never be made so poor, to have his house so rifled and spoiled, but there will remain much treasure within. If he has but a dish or a spoon or anything in the world in his house, there will be much treasure so long as he is there. There is the presence of God and the blessing of God upon him, and therein is much treasure. But in the revenues of the wicked there is trouble. There is more treasure in the poorest body's house, if he is godly, than in the house of the greatest man in the world, who has his fine hangings and finely-wrought beds and chairs and couches and cupboards of plate and the like. Whatever he has, he has not so much treasure in it as there is in the house of the poorest righteous soul.

It is no marvel, therefore, that Paul was content, for a verse or two after my text you read: 'But I have all and abound. I am full' (Philippians 4. 18). I have all? Alas, poor man! what did Paul have that could make him say he had all? Where was there ever a man more afflicted than Paul was? Many times he had not tatters to hang about his body to cover his nakedness. He had no bread to eat, he was often in nakedness, and put in the stocks and whipped and cruelly used, 'Yet I have all', says Paul, for all that. Yes, you will find it in 2 Corinthians: He professes there that he did possess all things: 'As sorrowful, yet always rejoicing; as poor, yet making many rich; as having nothing, and yet possessing all things' (2 Corinthians 6. 10). Mark what he says – it is, 'as having nothing' but it is 'possessing all things'. He does not say: 'As possessing all things', but 'possessing all things'. I have very little in the world, he says, but yet possessing all things. So you see that a Christian has cause to take pleasure in God's hand, whatever his hand may be.

VIII. The eighth thing in contentment is, Submitting, and taking pleasure *in God's disposal*.

That is to say, the soul that has learned this lesson of contentment looks up to God in all things. He does not look down at the instruments and means, so as to say that such a man did it, that it was the unreasonableness of such and such instruments, and similar barbarous usage by such and such; but he looks up to God. A contented heart looks to God's disposal, and submits to God's disposal, that is, he sees the wisdom of God in everything. In his submission he sees his sovereignty, but what makes him take pleasure is God's wisdom. The Lord knows how to order things better than I. The Lord sees further than I do; I only see things at present but the Lord sees a great while from now. And how do I know but that had it not been for this affliction, I should have been undone. I know that the love of God may as well stand with an afflicted condition as with a prosperous condition. There are reasonings of this kind in a contented spirit, submitting to the disposal of God.

IX. The last thing is, This is in *every condition*. Now we shall enlarge on this a little.

1. Submitting to God in whatever affliction befalls us: as to the kind of affliction.

2. As to the time and continuance of the affliction.

3. As to the variety and changes of affliction: Whatever they are, yet there must be a submission to God's disposal in every condition.

1. As to the *kind of affliction*. Many men and women will in general say that they must submit to God in affliction; I suppose that if you were to go now from one end of this congregation to the other, and speak thus to every soul: 'Would you not submit to God's disposal, in whatever condition he might place you?', you would say, 'God forbid that it should be otherwise!' But we have a saying, There is a great deal of deceit in general statements. In general, you would submit to anything; but what if it is in this or that particular case which crosses you most? – Then, anything but that! We are usually apt to think that any condition is better than that condition in which God has placed us. Now, this is not contentment; it should be not only to any condition in general, but for the kind of the affliction, including that which most crosses you. God, it may be, strikes you in your child – 'Oh, if

it had been in my possessions' you say, 'I would be content!' Perhaps he strikes you in your marriage. 'Oh,' you say, 'I would rather have been stricken in my health.' And if he had struck you in your health – 'Oh, then, if it had been in my trading, I would not have cared.' But we must not be our own carvers. Whatever particular afflictions God may place us in, we must be content in them.

2. There must be a submission to God in every affliction, *as to the time and continuance of the affliction*. 'Perhaps I could submit and be content', says someone, 'but this affliction has been on me a long time, three months, a year, many years, and I do not know how to yield and submit to it, my patience is worn out and broken.' It may even be a spiritual affliction – you could submit to God, you say, in any outward affliction, but not in a soul-affliction. Or if it were an affliction upon the soul, trouble upon the heart, if it were the withdrawing of God's face – 'Yet if this had been but for a little time I could submit; but to seek God for so long and still he does not appear, Oh how shall I bear this?' We must not be our own disposers for the *time* of deliverance any more than for the *kind* and *way* of deliverance.

I will give you a Scripture or two about this. That we are to submit to God for the time as well as the kind of affliction, see the latter end of the first chapter of Ezekiel: 'When I saw it I fell upon my face, and I heard a voice of one that spake.' The Prophet was cast down upon his face, but how long must he lie upon his face? 'And he said unto me, Son of man, stand upon thy feet and I will speak unto thee. And the spirit entered into me, when he spake unto me, and set me upon my feet.' Ezekiel was cast down upon his face, and there he must lie till God should bid him to stand up; yea, and not only so, but till God's Spirit came into him and enabled him to stand up. So when God casts us down, we must be content to lie till God bids us stand up, and God's Spirit enters into us to enable us to stand up. You know how Noah was put into the Ark – certainly he knew there was much affliction in the Ark, with all kinds of creatures shut up with him for twelve months together

–it was a mighty thing, yet God having shut him up, even though the waters were assuaged, Noah was not to come out of the Ark till God bid him. So though we be shut up in great afflictions, and we may think of this and that and the other means to come out of that affliction, yet till God opens the door, we should be willing to stay; God has put us in, and God will bring us out. So we read in the Acts of Paul, when they had shut him in prison and would have sent for him out; 'No', says Paul, 'they shut us in, let them come and fetch us out.' So in a holy, gracious way should a soul say, 'Well, this affliction that I am brought into, is by the hand of God, and I am content to be here till God brings me out himself.' God requires it at our hands, that we should not be willing to come out till he comes and fetches us out.

In Joshua 4. 10 there is a remarkable story that may serve our purpose very well: We read of the priests that they bore the ark and stood in the midst of Jordan (you know when the Children of Israel went into the land of Canaan they went through the river Jordan). Now to go through the river Jordan was a very dangerous thing, but God had told them to go. They might have been afraid of the water coming in upon them. But mark, it is said, 'The priests that bare the ark stood in the midst of Jordan till every thing was finished that the Lord commanded Joshua to speak unto the people, according to all that Moses commanded Joshua, and the people hasted and passed over: And it came to pass when all the people were clean passed over, that the ark of the Lord passed over, and the priests in the presence of the people.' Now it was God's disposal that all the people should pass over first, that they should be safe on land; but the priests must stand still till all the people had passed over, and then they must have leave to go. But they must stay till God would have them to go, stay in all that danger! For certainly, to reason and sense, there was a great deal of danger in staying, for the text says that the people hasted over, but the priests they must stay till the people have gone, stay till God calls them out from that place of danger. And so many times it proves the case that God is pleased to dispose of things so that his ministers must stay longer in danger than the people, and likewise magistrates and those in public places, which should make people to be satisfied and contented with a lower position into which God has put them. Though your position is low, yet you are not in the same danger as those who are in a higher position. God calls those in public positions to stand longer in the gap and place of danger than other people, but we must be content to stay even in Jordan till the Lord shall be pleased to call us out.

3. And then for *the variety of our condition*. We must be content with the particular affliction, and the time, and all the circumstances about the affliction – for sometimes the circumstances are greater afflictions than the afflictions themselves – and for the variety. God may exercise us with various afflictions one after another, as has been very noticeable, even of late, that many who have been plundered and come away, afterwards have fallen sick and died; they had fled for their lives and afterwards the plague has come among them; and if not that affliction, it may be some other. It is very rarely that one affliction comes alone; commonly, afflictions are not single things, but they come one upon the neck of another. God may strike one man in his possessions, then in his body, then in his name, wife, child or dear friend, and so it comes in a variety of ways; it is the way of God ordinarily (you may find it by experience) that one affliction seldom comes alone. Now this is hard, when one affliction follows after another, when there is a variety of afflictions, when there is a mighty change in one's condition, up and down, this way, and that: there indeed is the trial of a Christian. Now there must be submission to God's disposal in them. I remember it was said even of Cato, who was a Heathen, that no man saw him to be changed, though he lived in a time when the commonwealth was so often changed; yet it is said of him, he was the same still, though his condition was changed, and he passed through a variety of conditions. Oh that the same could be said of many Christians, that though their circumstances are changed, yet that nobody could see them changed, they are the same!

Did you see what a gracious, sweet and holy temper they were in before? They are in it still. Thus are we to submit to the disposal of God in every condition.

Contentment is the inward, quiet, gracious frame of spirit, freely submitting to and taking pleasure in God's disposal in every condition: That is the description, and in it nine distinct things have been opened up which we summarize as follows: First, that contentment is a heart-work within the soul; Secondly, it is the quieting of the heart; Thirdly, it is the frame of the spirit; Fourthly, it is a gracious frame; Fifthly, it is the free working of this gracious frame; Sixthly, there is in it a submission to God, sending the soul under God; Seventhly, there is a taking pleasure in the hand of God; Eighthly, all is traced to God's disposal; Ninthly, in every condition, however hard it be and however long it continue.

Now those of you who have learned to be content, have learned to attain to these various things. I hope that the very opening of these things may so far work on your hearts that you may lay your hands upon your hearts on what has been said, I say, that the very telling you what the lesson is may cause you to lay your hands on your hearts and say, 'Lord, I see there is more to Christian contentment than I thought there was, and I have been far from learning this lesson. Indeed, I have only learned my ABC in this lesson of contentment. I am only in the lower form in Christ's school if I am in it at all.' We shall speak of these things more later, but my particular aim in opening this point is to show what a great mystery there is in Christian contentment, and how many distinct lessons there are to be learned, that we may come to attain to this heavenly disposition, to which St Paul attained.

2

THE MYSTERY OF CONTENTMENT

But you will object: What you speak of is very good, if we could attain to it; but is it possible for anyone to attain to this? It is possible if you get skill in the art of it; you may attain to it, and it will prove to be not such a difficult thing either, if you but understand the mystery of it. There are many things that men do in their callings, that if a countryman comes and sees, he thinks it a mighty hard thing, and that he should never be able to do it. But that is because he does not understand the art of it; there is a twist of the hand by which you may do it with ease. Now that is the business of this book, to open to you the art and mystery of contentment.

There is a great mystery and art in what way a Christian comes to contentment. By what has been already opened to you there will appear some mystery and art, as that a man should be content with his affliction, and yet thoroughly sensible of his affliction too; to be thoroughly sensible of an affliction, and to endeavour to remove it by all lawful means, and yet to be content: there is a mystery in that. How to join these two together: to be sensible of an affliction as much as a man or woman who is not content; I am sensible of it as fully as they, and I seek ways to be delivered from it as well as they, and yet still my heart abides content – this is, I say, a mystery, that is very hard for a carnal heart to understand. But grace teaches such a mixture, teaches us how to make a mixture of sorrow and a mixture of joy together; and that makes contentment, the mingling of joy and sorrow, of gracious joy and gracious sorrow together. Grace teaches us how to moderate and to order an affliction so that there shall be a sense of it, and yet for all that contentment under it.

There are several things for opening the mystery of contentment.

I. The first thing is, To show that there is a great mystery in it. It may be said of one who is contented in a Christian way that *he is the most contented man in the world, and yet the most unsatisfied man in the world*; these two together must needs be mysterious. I say, a contented man, just as he is the most contented, so he is the most unsatisfied man in the world. You never learned the mystery of contentment unless it may be said of you that, just as you are the most contented man, so you are also the most unsatisfied man in the world.

You will say, 'How is that?' A man who has learned the art of contentment is the most contented with any low condition that he has in the world, and yet he cannot be satisfied with the enjoyment of all the world. He is contented if he has but a crust, but bread and water, that is, if God disposes of him, for the things of the world, to have but bread and water for his present condition, he can be satisfied with God's disposal in that; yet if God should give unto him Kingdoms and Empires, all the world to rule, if he should give it him for his portion, he would not be satisfied with that. Here is the mystery of it: though his heart is so enlarged that the enjoyment of all the world and ten thousand worlds cannot satisfy him for his portion; yet he has a heart quieted under God's disposal, if he gives him but bread and water. To join these two together must needs be a great art and mystery. Though he is contented with God in a little, yet those things that would content other men will not content him. The men of the world seek after wealth, and think if they had thus much, and thus much, they would be content. They do not aim at great things; but if I had, perhaps some man thinks, only two or three hundred a year, then I should be well enough; if I had but a hundred a year, or a thousand a year, says another, then I should be satisfied. But a gracious heart says that if he had ten hundred thousand times so much a year, it would not satisfy him; if he had the quintessence of all the excellences of all the creatures in the world, it could not satisfy him; and yet this man can sing, and be merry and joyful when he has only a crust of bread and a little water in the world. Surely religion is a great mystery! Great is the mystery of godliness, not only in the doctrinal part of it, but in the practical part of it also.

Godliness teaches us this mystery, Not to be satisfied with all the world for our portion, and yet to be content with the meanest condition in which we are. When Luther was sent great gifts by Dukes and Princes, he refused them, and he says, 'I did vehemently protest that God should not put me off so; 'tis not that which will content me.' A little in the world will content a Christian for his passage. Mark, here lies the mystery of it, A little in the world will content a Christian for his passage, but all the world, and ten thousand times more, will not content a Christian for his portion. A carnal heart will be content with these things of the world for his portion; and that is the difference between a carnal heart and a gracious heart. But a gracious heart says, 'Lord, do with me what you will for my passage through this world; I will be content with that, but I cannot be content with all the world for my portion.' So there is the mystery of true contentment. A contented man, though he is most contented with the least things in the world, yet he is the most dissatisfied man that lives in the world.

A soul that is capable of God can be filled with nothing else but God; nothing but God can fill a soul that is capable of God. Though a gracious heart knows that it is capable of God, and was made for God, carnal hearts think without reference to God. But a gracious heart, being enlarged to be capable of God, and enjoying somewhat of him, can be filled by nothing in the world; it must only be God himself. Therefore you will observe, that whatever God may give to a gracious heart, a heart that is godly, unless he gives himself it will not do. A godly heart will not only have the mercy, but the God of that

[43]

mercy as well; and then a little matter is enough in the world, so be it he has the God of the mercy which he enjoys. In Philippians 4. 7, 9 (I need go no further to show clear Scripture for this) compare verse 7 with verse 9: 'And the peace of God which passeth all understanding shall keep your hearts and minds through Jesus Christ.' The peace of God shall keep your hearts. Then in verse 9: 'Those things which ye have both learned, and received, and heard, and seen in me, do: and the God of peace shall be with you.' The peace of God shall keep you, and the God of peace shall be with you. Here is what I would observe from this text, That the peace of God is not enough to a gracious heart except it may have the God of that peace. A carnal heart could be satisfied if he might but have outward peace, though it is not the peace of God; peace in the state, and his trading, would satisfy him. But mark how a godly heart goes beyond a carnal. All outward peace is not enough; I must have the peace of God. But suppose you have the peace of God, Will that not quiet you? No, I must have the God of peace; as the peace of God so the God of peace. That is, I must enjoy that God who gives me the peace; I must have the Cause as well as the effect. I must see from whence my peace comes, and enjoy the Fountain of my peace, as well as the stream of my peace. And so in other mercies: have I health from God? I must have the God of my health to be my portion, or else I am not satisfied. It is not life, but the God of my life; it is not riches, but the God of those riches, that I must have, the God of my preservation, as well as my preservation.

A gracious heart is not satisfied without this: to have the God of the mercy, as well as the mercy. In Psalm 73. 25, 'Whom have I in heaven but thee, and there is none upon the earth that I desire beside thee.' There is nothing in heaven or earth that can satisfy me, but yourself. If God gave you not only earth but heaven, that you should rule over sun, moon and stars, and have the rule over the highest of the sons of men, it would not be enough to satisfy you, unless you had God himself. There lies the first mystery of contentment. And truly a contented man, though he is the most contented man

[44]

in the world, is the most dissatisfied man in the world; that is, those things that will satisfy the world, will not satisfy him.

II. *A Christian comes to contentment, not so much by way of addition, as by way of subtraction.* That is his way of contentment, and it is a way that the world has no skill in. I open it thus: not so much by adding to what he would have, or to what he has, not by adding more to his condition; but rather by subtracting from his desires, so as to make his desires and his circumstances even and equal. A carnal heart knows no way to be contented but this: I have such and such possessions, and if I had this added to them, and the other comfort added that I have not now, then I should be contented. Perhaps I have lost my possessions, if I could only have given to me something to make up my loss, then I should be a contented man. But contentment does not come in that way, it does not come, I say, by adding to what you want, but by subtracting from your desires. It is all one to a Christian, whether I get up to what I would have, or get my desires down to what I have, either to attain what I do desire, or to bring down my desires to what I have already attained. My wealth is the same, for it is as fitting for me to bring my desire down to my circumstances, as it is to raise up my circumstances to my desire.

Now I say that a heart that has no grace, and is not instructed in this mystery of contentment, knows of no way to get contentment, but to have his possessions raised up to his desires; but the Christian has another way to contentment, that is, he can bring his desires down to his possessions, and so he attains his contentment. Thus the Lord fashions the hearts of the children of men. If the heart of a man is fashioned to his circumstances, he may have as much contentment as if his circumstances were fashioned to his heart. Some men have a mighty large heart, but they have straitened circumstances, and they can never have contentment when their hearts are big and their circumstances are little. But though a man cannot bring his circumstances to be as great as his heart, yet if he can bring his heart to be as little as his circumstances, to make them even, this is the way to contentment. The world

[45]

is infinitely deceived in thinking that contentment lies in having more than we already have. Here lies the bottom and root of all contentment, when there is an evenness and proportion between our hearts and our circumstances. That is why many godly men who are in a low position live more sweet and comfortable lives than those who are richer. Contentment is not always clothed with silk and purple and velvets, but it is sometimes in a home-spun suit, in mean circumstances, as well as in higher. Many men who once have had great estates, and God has brought them into a lower position have had more contentment in those circumstances than they had before. Now how can that possibly be? Quite easily, if you only understood that the root of contentment consists in the suitableness and proportion of a man's spirit to his possessions, an evenness where one end is not longer and bigger than the other. The heart is contented and there is comfort in those circumstances. But now let God give a man riches, no matter how great, yet if the Lord gives him up to the pride of his heart, he will never be contented: on the other hand, let God bring anyone into mean circumstances, and then let God but fashion and suit his heart to those circumstances and he will be content.

It is the same in walking: Suppose a man had a very long leg, and his other leg was short – why, though one of his legs was longer than usual, still he could not go as well as a man both of whose legs are shorter than his. I would compare a long leg, when one is longer than the other, to a man who has a high position and is very rich and a great man in the world, but he has a very proud heart, too, and that is longer and larger than his position. This man cannot but be troubled in his circumstances. Another man is in a mean position, his circumstances are low and his heart is low too, so that his heart and his circumstances are even. This man walks with abundantly more ease than the other. Thus a gracious heart thinks in this way: 'The Lord has been pleased to bring down my circumstances; now if the Lord brings down my heart and makes it equal to my circumstances, then I am well enough.'

So when God brings down his circumstances, he does not so much labour to raise up his circumstances again as to bring his heart down to his circumstances. Even the heathen philosophers had a little glimpse of this: they could say that the best riches is poverty of desires – those are the words of a heathen. That is, if a man or woman have their desires cut short, and have no large desires, that man or woman is rich. So this is the art of contentment: not to seek to add to our circumstances, but to subtract from our desires. Another author has said, The way to be rich is not by increasing wealth, but by diminishing our desires. Certainly that man or woman is rich, who have their desires satisfied. Now a contented man has his desires satisfied, God satisfies them, that is, all considered, he is satisfied that his circumstances are for the present the best circumstances. So he comes to this contentment by way of subtraction, and not addition.

III. *A Christian comes to contentment, not so much by getting rid of the burden that is on him, as by adding another burden to himself.* This is a way that flesh and blood has little skill in. You will say, 'How is this?' In this manner: are you afflicted, and is there a great load and burden on you because of your affliction? You think there is no way in the world to get contentment, but, O that this burden were but off! O it is a heavy load, and few know what a burden I have. What, do you think that there is no way for the contentment of your spirit, but to get rid of your burden? O you are deceived. The way of contentment is to add another burden, that is, to labour to load and burden your heart with your sin; the heavier tne burden of your sin is to your heart, the lighter will the burden of your affliction be to your heart, and so you shall come to be content. If your burden were lightened, that would content you; you think there is no way to lighten it but to get it off. But you are deceived; for if you can get your heart to be more burdened with your sin, you will be less burdened with your afflictions.

You will say, this is a strange way for a man or woman to get ease to their condition, to lay a greater burden upon them when they are already burdened? You think there is no other way, when you are afflicted, but to be jolly and merry, and get into company. Oh no, you are deceived, your burden will come again. Alas, this is a poor way to get one's spirit quieted; poor man, the burden will be upon him again. If you would have your burden light, get alone and examine your heart for your sin, and charge your soul with your sin. If your burden is in your possessions, for the abuse of them, or if it is a burden upon your body, for the abuse of your health and strength, and the abuse of any mercies that now the Lord has taken away from you, that you have not honoured God with those mercies that you have had, but you have walked wantonly and carelessly; if you so fall to bemoaning your sin before the Lord, you shall quickly find the burden of your affliction to be lighter than it was before. Do but try this piece of skill and art, to get your souls contented with any low circumstances that God puts you into.

Many times in a family, when any affliction befalls them, Oh, what an amount of discontent is there between man and wife! If they are crossed in their possessions at land, or have bad news from across the seas, or if those whom they trusted are ruined and the like, or perhaps something in the family causes strife between man and wife, in reference to the children or servants, and there is nothing but quarrelling and discontent among them, now they are many times burdened with their own discontent; and perhaps will say one to another, It is very uncomfortable for us to live so discontented as we do. But have you ever tried this way, husband and wife? Have you ever got alone and said, 'Come, Oh let us go and humble our souls before God together, let us go into our chamber and humble our souls before God for our sin, by which we have abused those mercies that God has taken away from us, and we have provoked God against us. Oh let us charge ourselves with our sin, and be humbled before the Lord together.'? Have you tried such a way as this? Oh you would find that the cloud would be taken away, and the sun would shine in upon you, and you would have a great deal more contentment than ever you had. If a man's estate is broken, either by plunderers, or any other way; how shall this man have contentment? How? By the breaking of his heart. God has broken your estate; Oh seek to him for the breaking of your heart likewise. Indeed, a broken estate and a whole heart, a hard heart, will not join together; there will be no contentment. But a broken estate and a broken heart will so suit one another, as that there will be more contentment than there was before. Add therefore to the breaking of your estate, the breaking of your heart, and that is the way to be contented in a Christian manner, which is the third mystery in Christian contentment.

IV. *It is not so much the removing of the affliction that is upon us as the changing of the affliction, the metamorphosing of the affliction, so that it is quite turned and changed into something else.* I mean in regard of the use of it, though for the thing itself the affliction remains. The way of contentment to a carnal heart is only the removing of the affliction. O that it may be gone! 'No', says a gracious heart, 'God has taught me a way to be content though the affliction itself still continues.' There is a power of grace to turn this affliction into good; it takes away the sting and poison of it. Take the case of poverty, a man's possessions are lost: Well, is there no way to be contented till your possessions are made up again? Till your poverty is removed? Yes, certainly, Christianity would teach contentment, though poverty continues. It will teach you how to turn your poverty to spiritual riches. You shall be poor still as to your outward possessions, but this shall be altered; whereas before it was a natural evil to you, it comes now to be turned to a spiritual benefit to you. And so you come to be content.

There is a saying of Ambrose, 'Even poverty itself is riches to holy men.' Godly men make their poverty turn to riches; they get more riches out of their poverty than ever they get out of their revenues. Out of all their trading in this world they never had such incomes as they have had out of their poverty. This a carnal heart will think strange, that a man shall make poverty the most gainful trade that ever he had in the world. I am persuaded that many Christians have found it so, that they have got more good by their poverty, than ever they got by all their riches. You find it in Scripture. Therefore think not this strange that I am speaking of. You do not find one godly man who came out of an affliction worse than when he went into it; though for a while he was shaken, yet at last he was better for an affliction. But a great many godly men, you find, have been worse for their prosperity. Scarcely one godly man that you read of in Scripture but was worse for prosperity (except Daniel and Nehemiah – I do not read of any hurt they got by their prosperity); scarcely, I think, is there one example of a godly man who was not worse for his prosperity than better. So rather you see it is no strange thing to one who is gracious that they shall get good by their affliction.

Luther has a similar expression in his comment on the 5th chapter of the Galatians, the 17th verse: he says, 'A Christian becomes a mighty worker and a wonderful creator, that is', he says, 'to create out of heaviness joy, out of terror comfort, out of sin righteousness, and out of death life.' He brings light out of darkness. It was God's prerogative and great power, his creating power to command the light to shine out of darkness. Now a Christian is partaker of the divine nature, so the Scripture says; grace is part of the divine nature, and, being part of the divine nature, it has an impression of God's omnipotent power, that is, to create light out of darkness, to bring good out of evil – by this way a Christian comes to be content. God has given a Christian such power that he can turn afflictions into mercies, can turn darkness into light. If a man had the power that Christ had, when the water pots were filled, he could by a word turn the water into wine. If you who have nothing but water to drink had the power to turn it into wine, then you might be contented; certainly a Christian has received this power from God, to work thus miraculously. It is the nature of grace to turn water into wine, that is, to turn the water of your affliction, into the wine of heavenly consolation.

If you understand this in a carnal way, I know it will be

ridiculous for a minister to speak thus to you, and many carnal people are ready to make such expressions as these ridiculous, understanding them in a carnal way. This is just like Nicodemus, in the third of John, 'What! can a man be born when he is old? can he enter the second time into his mother's womb and be born?' So when we say of grace, that it can turn water into wine, and turn poverty into riches, and make poverty a gainful trade, a carnal heart says, 'Let them have that trade if they will, and let them have water to drink, and see if they can turn it into wine.' Oh, take heed you do not speak in a scornful way of the ways of God; grace has the power to turn afflictions into mercies. Two men may have the same affliction; to one it shall be as gall and wormwood, yet it shall be wine and honey and delightfulness and joy and advantage and riches to the other. This is the mystery of contentment, not so much by removing the evil, as by metamorphosing the evil, by changing the evil into good.

V. *A Christian comes to this contentment not by making up the wants of his circumstances, but by the performance of the work of his circumstances.* This is the way of contentment. There are these circumstances that I am in, with many wants: I want this and the other comfort – well, how shall I come to be satisfied and content? A carnal heart thinks, I must have my wants made up or else it is impossible that I should be content. But a gracious heart says, 'What is the duty of the circumstances God has put me into? Indeed, my circumstances have changed, I was not long since in a prosperous state, but God has changed my circumstances. The Lord has called me no more Naomi, but Marah. Now what am I to do? What can I think now are those duties that God requires of me in the circumstances that he has now put me into? Let me exert my strength to perform the duties of my present circumstances. Others spend their thoughts on things that disturb and disquiet them, and so they grow more and more discontented. Let me spend my thoughts in thinking what my duty is, what is the duty of my present circumstances which I am in?' 'O', says a man whose condition is changed and who has lost his wealth, 'Had I but my wealth, as I had heretofore, how would I use it to his glory? God has made me see that I did not honour him with my possessions as I ought to have done. O if I had it again, I would do better than I did before.' But this may be but a temptation. You should rather think, 'What does God require of me in the circumstances I am now brought into?' You should labour to bring your heart to quiet and contentment by setting your soul to work in the duties of your present condition. And the truth is, I know nothing more effective for quieting a Christian soul and getting contentment than this, setting your heart to work in the duties of the immediate circumstances that you are now in, and taking heed of your thoughts about other conditions as a mere temptation.

I cannot better compare the folly of those men and women who think they will get contentment by musing about other circumstances than to the way of children: perhaps they have climbed a hill and look a good way off and see another hill, and they think if they were on the top of that, they would be able to touch the clouds with their fingers; but when they are on the top of that hill, alas, they are as far from the clouds as they were before. So it is with many who think, If I were in such circumstances, then I should have contentment; and perhaps they get into those circumstances, and they are as far from contentment as before. But then they think that if they were in other circumstances, they would be contented, but when they have got into those circumstances, they are still as far from contentment as before. No, no, let me consider what is the duty of my present circumstances, and content my heart with this, and say, 'Well, though I am in a low position, yet I am serving the counsels of God in those circumstances where I am; it is the counsel of God that has brought me into these circumstances that I am in, and I desire to serve the counsel of God in these circumstances.'

There is a remarkable Scripture concerning David, of whom it is said that he served his generation: 'After David had served his generation according to the will of God, then he slept.' It is a saying of Paul concerning him in Acts 13. 36. In your Bibles it is, 'After he had served his own generation according to the will of God', but the word that is translated *will*, means the counsel of God, and so it may be translated as well, 'That after David in his generation had served God's counsel, then he fell asleep'. We ordinarily take the words thus, That David served his generation: that is, he did the work of his generation – that is to serve a man's generation. But it is clearer if you read it thus, After David in his generation had served the counsel of God, then David fell asleep. O that should be the care of a Christian, to serve out God's counsels. What is the counsel of God? The circumstances that I am in, God has put me into by his own counsel, the counsel of his own will. Now I must serve God's counsel in my generation; whatever is the counsel of God in my circumstances, I must be careful to serve that. So I shall have my heart quieted for the present, and shall live and die peaceably and comfortably, if I am careful to serve God's counsel.

VI. *A gracious heart is contented by the melting of his will and desires into God's will and desires; by this means he gets contentment.* This too is a mystery to a carnal heart. It is not by having his own desires satisfied, but by melting his will and desires into God's will. So that, in one sense, he comes to have his desires satisfied though he does not obtain the thing that he desired before; still he comes to be satisfied with this, because he makes his will to be at one with God's will. This is a small degree higher than submitting to the will of God. You all say that you should submit to God's will; a Christian has got beyond this. He can make God's will and his own the same. It is said of believers that they are joined to the Lord, and are one spirit; that means, that whatever God's will is, I do not only see good reason to submit to it, but God's will is my will. When the soul can make over, as it were, its will to God, it must needs be contented. Others would fain get the thing they desire, but a gracious heart will say, 'O what God would have, I would have too; I will not only yield to it, but I would have it too.'

A gracious heart has learned this art, not only to make the

commanding will of God to be its own will – that is, what God commands me to do, I will do it – but to make the providential will of God and the operative will of God to be his will too. God commands this thing, which perhaps you who are Christians may have some skill in, but whatever God works you must will, as well as what God commands. You must make God's providential will and his operative will, your will as well as God's will, and in this way you must come to contentment. A Christian makes over his will to God, and in making over his will to God, he has no other will but God's. Suppose a man were to make over his debt to another man. If the man to whom I owe the debt be satisfied and contented, I am satisfied because I have made it over to him, and I need not be discontented and say, 'My debt is not paid and I am not satisfied'. Yes, you are satisfied, for he to whom you made over your debt is satisfied. It is just the same, for all the world, between God and a Christian: a Christian heart makes over his will to God: now then if God's will is satisfied, then I am satisfied, for I have no will of my own, it is melted into the will of God. That is the excellence of grace: grace does not only subject the will to God, but it melts the will into God's will, so that they are now but one will. What a sweet satisfaction the soul must have in this condition, when all is made over to God. You will say, This is hard! I will express it a little more: A gracious heart must needs have satisfaction in this way, because godliness teaches him this, to see that his good is more in God than in himself. The good of my life and comforts and my happiness and my glory and my riches are more in God than in myself. We may perhaps speak more of that, when we come to the lessons that are to be learned. It is by this that a gracious heart gets contentment; he melts his will into God's, for he says, 'If God has glory, I have glory; God's glory is my glory, and therefore God's will is mine; if God has riches, then I have riches; if God is magnified, then I am magnified; if God is satisfied, then I am satisfied; God's wisdom and holiness is mine, and therefore his will must needs be mine, and my will must needs be his.' This is the art of a Christian's contentment: he melts his will into the will of God, and makes over his will to God: 'Oh Lord, thou shalt choose our inheritance for us' (Psalm 47. 4).

VII. *The mystery consists not in bringing anything from outside to make my condition more comfortable, but in purging out something that is within.* Now the men of the world, when they would have contentment, and lack anything, Oh, they must have something from outside to content them. But a godly man says: 'Let me get something out that is in already, and then I shall come to contentment.' Suppose a man has a fever, that makes what he drinks taste bitter: he says, 'You must put some sugar into my drink'; his wife puts some in, and still the drink tastes bitter. Why? Because the bitterness comes from a bitter choleric humour within. But let the physician come and give him a bitter potion to purge out the bitterness that is within, and then he can taste his drink well enough. It is just the same with the men of the world: Oh such circumstances are bitter, and if I could have such and such a mercy added to this mercy, then it would be sweet; but even if God should put a spoonful or two of sugar in, it would still be bitter. The way to contentment is to purge out your lusts and bitter humours. 'From whence are wars, and strifes? are they not from your lusts that are within you?' (James 4. 1). They are not so much from things outside, but from within. I have said sometimes, 'Not all the storms that are abroad can make an earthquake, but the vapours that have got within.' So if those lusts that are within, in your heart, were got out, your condition would be a contented condition. These are the mysterious ways of godliness, that the men of the world never think of. When did you ever think of such a way as this, to go and purge out the diseases of your heart that are within?

Here are seven particulars now named, and there are many more. Without the understanding of these things, and the practice of them, you will never come to a true contentment in your life; Oh, you will be bunglers in this trade of Christianity. But the right perceiving of these things will help you to be instructed in it, as in a mystery.

3

THE MYSTERY OF CONTENTMENT – *continued*

The mystery of contentment may be shown even more. A gracious heart gets contentment in a mysterious way, a way that the world is not acquainted with.

VIII. *He lives upon the dew of God's blessing.* Adrian Junius uses the simile of a grasshopper to describe a contented man, and says he has this motto, 'I am content with what I have, and hope for better.' A grasshopper leaps and skips up and down, and lives on the dew. A grasshopper does not live on the grass as other things do; you do not know what it feeds on. Other things though as little as grasshoppers, feed upon seeds or little flies and such things, but as for the grasshopper, you do not know what it feeds upon. In the same way a Christian can get food that the world does not know of; he is fed in a secret way by the dew of the blessing of God. A poor man or woman who has but a little with grace, lives a more contented life than his rich neighbour who has a great income; we find it so ordinarily – though they have but a little, yet they have a secret blessing of God with it, which they cannot express to anyone else. If you were to come to them and say: 'How is it that you live as happily as you do?', they cannot tell you what they have; but they find there is a sweetness in what they do enjoy, and they know by experience that they never had such sweetness in former times. Even though they had a greater abundance in former times than they have now, yet they know they never had such sweetness; but how this comes about they cannot tell. We may mention some considerations, in what godly men enjoy, which make their condition sweet.

For example, Take these four or five considerations with which a godly man finds contentment in what he has, though it is ever so little.

1. *Because in what he has, he has the love of God to him*. If a king were to send a piece of meat from his own table, it would be a great deal more pleasant to a courtier than if he had twenty dishes as an ordinary allowance; if the king sends even a little thing and says, 'Go and carry it to that man as a token of my love', Oh, how delightful would that be to him! When your husbands are at sea and send you a token of their love, it is worth more than forty times what you already have in your houses. Every good thing the people of God enjoy, they enjoy it in God's love, as a token of God's love, and coming from God's eternal love to them, and this must needs be very sweet to them.

2. *What they have is sanctified to them for good*. Other men have what they enjoy in the way of common providence, but the saints have it in a special way. Others have what they have and no more: meat, and drink, and houses, and clothes, and money, and that is all. But a gracious heart finds contentment in this, I have it, and I have a sanctified use of it too; I find God goes along with what I have to draw my heart nearer to him, and sanctify my heart to him. If I find my heart drawn nearer to God by what I enjoy, that is much more than if I have it without any sanctifying of my heart by it. There is a secret dew that goes along with it: the dew of God's love in it, and the dew of sanctification.

3. *A gracious heart has what he has free of cost; he is not likely to be called to pay for it*. The difference between what a godly man has and a wicked man, is this: A godly man is as a child in an inn, an inn-keeper has his child in the house, and provides his diet, and lodging, and what is needful for him. Now a stranger comes, and he has dinner and supper provided, and lodging, but the stranger must pay for everything. It may be that the child's fare is meaner than the fare of the stranger;

the stranger has boiled and roast and baked, but he must pay for it, there must come a reckoning for it. Just so it is: many of God's people have only mean fare, but God as a Father provides it, and it is free of cost, they need not pay for what they have, it is paid for before; but the wicked in all their pomp, and pride, and finery: they have what they ask for, but there must come a reckoning for everything, they must pay for all at the conclusion, and is it not better to have a little free of cost, than to have to pay for everything? Grace shows a man that what he has, he has free of cost, from God as from a Father, and therefore it must needs be very sweet.

4. A godly man may very well be content, though he has only a little, *for what he does have he has by right of Jesus Christ, by the purchase of Jesus Christ.* He has a right to it, a different kind of right to that which a wicked man can have to what he has. Wicked men have certain outward things; I do not say they are usurpers of what they have; they have a right to it, and that before God, but how? It is a right by mere donation, that is, God by his free bounty gives it to them; but the right that the saints have is a right of purchase: it is paid for, and it is their own, and they may in a holy manner and holy way claim whatever they have need of. We cannot express the difference between the right of a holy man, and the right of the wicked more fully than by the following simile: a criminal is condemned to die, and yet by favour he has his supper provided overnight. Now though the criminal has forfeited all his right to all things, to every bit of bread, yet if he is given his supper he does not steal it. This is true though he has forfeited all rights by his fault, and after he has once been condemned he has no right to anything. So it is with the wicked: they have forfeited all their right to the comforts of this world, they are condemned by God as criminals, and are going to execution; but if God in his bounty gives them something to preserve them here in the world, they cannot be said to be thieves or robbers. But if a man is given a supper overnight before his execution, is that like the supper that he was wont to have in his own house, when he ate his own bread,

and had his wife and children about him? Oh, a dish of green herbs at home would be a great deal better than any dainties in such a supper as that. But a child of God has not a right merely by donation; what he has is his own, through the purchase of Christ. Every bit of bread you eat, if you are a godly man or woman, Jesus Christ has bought it for you. You go to market and buy your meat and drink with your money, but know that before you buy it, or pay money, Christ has bought it at the hand of God the Father with his blood. You have it at the hands of men for money, but Christ has bought it at the hand of his Father by his blood. Certainly it is a great deal better and sweeter now, though it is but a little.

5. There is another thing that shows the sweetness that is in the little that the Saints have, by which they come to have contentment, whereas others cannot, that is, *Every little that they have is but as an earnest penny* for all the glory that is reserved for them; it is given them by God as the forerunner of those eternal mercies that the Lord intends for them*. Now if a man has but twelve pence given to him as an earnest penny for some great possession that he must have, is that not better than if he had forty pounds given to him otherwise? So every comfort that the saints have in this world is an earnest penny to them of those eternal mercies that the Lord has provided for them. Just as every affliction that the wicked have here is but the beginning of sorrows, and forerunner of those eternal sorrows that they are likely to have hereafter in Hell, so every comfort you have is a forerunner of those eternal mercies you shall have with God in Heaven. Not only are the consolations of God's Spirit the forerunners of those eternal comforts you shall have in Heaven, but when you sit at your table, and rejoice with your wife and children and friends, you may look upon every one of those but as a forerunner, yea the very earnest penny of eternal life to you. Now if this is so, it is no marvel that a Christian is contented, but this is a mystery to the wicked. I have what I have from the love of God, and I have it sanctified to me by God, and I have it free of cost from

* A first instalment which guarantees that the rest is to follow.

God by the purchase of the blood of Jesus Christ, and I have it as a forerunner of those eternal mercies that are reserved for me; and in this my soul rejoices. There is a secret dew of God's goodness and blessing upon him in his estate that others have not. By all this you may see the meaning of that Scripture, 'Better is a little with righteousness than great revenues without right' (Proverbs 16. 8). A man who has but a little, yet if he has it with righteousness, it is better than a great deal without right, yea, better than the great revenues of the wicked – so you have it in another Scripture. That is the next thing in Christian contentment: the mystery is in this, that he lives on the dew of God's blessing, in all the good things that he enjoys.

IX. *Not only in good things does a Christian have the dew of God's blessing, and find them very sweet to him, but in all the afflictions, all the evils that befall him, he can see love, and can enjoy the sweetness of love in his afflictions as well as in his mercies.* The truth is that the afflictions of God's people come from the same eternal love that Jesus Christ came from. Jerome said, 'He is a happy man who is beaten when the stroke is a stroke of love.' All God's strokes are strokes of love and mercy, all God's ways are mercy and truth, to those that fear him and love him (Psalm 25. 10). The ways of God, the ways of affliction, as well as the ways of prosperity, are mercy and love to him. Grace gives a man an eye, a piercing eye to pierce into the counsel of God, those eternal counsels of God for good to him, even in his afflictions; he can see the love of God in every affliction as well as in prosperity. Now this is a mystery to a carnal heart. They can see no such thing; perhaps they think God loves them when he prospers them and makes them rich, but they think God loves them not when he afflicts them. That is a mystery, but grace instructs men in that mystery, grace enables men to see love in the very frown of God's face, and so comes to receive contentment.

X. A godly man has contentment as a mystery, *because just as he sees all his afflictions come from the same love that Jesus Christ did, so he sees them all sanctified in Jesus Christ, sanctified in a Mediator*. He sees, I say, all the sting and venom and poison of them taken out by the virtue of Jesus Christ, the Mediator between God and man. For instance, when a Christian would have contentment he works it out thus: what is my affliction? Is it poverty that God strikes me with? – Jesus Christ had not a house to hide his head in, the fowls of the air had nests, and the foxes holes, but the Son of man had not a hole to hide his head in; now my poverty is sanctified by Christ's poverty. I can see by faith the curse and sting and venom taken out of my poverty by the poverty of Jesus Christ. Christ Jesus was poor in this world to deliver me from the curse of my poverty. So my poverty is not afflictive, if I can be contented in such a condition. That is the way, not to stand and repine, because I have not what others have; no, but I am poor, and Christ was poor, that he might bless my poverty to me.

And so again, am I disgraced or dishonoured? Is my good name taken away? Why, Jesus Christ had dishonour put upon him; he was called Beelzebub, and a Samaritan, and they said he had a devil in him. All the foul aspersions that could be, were cast upon Jesus Christ, and this was for me, that I might have the disgrace that is cast upon me sanctified to me. Whereas another man's heart is overwhelmed with dishonour, and disgrace, and he seeks in this way to get contentment: perhaps you have been spoken ill of and you have no other way to ease and right yourselves, but if they abuse you, you will abuse them back; and so you think to ease yourselves. Oh, but a Christian has another way to ease himself: others abuse and speak ill of me, but did they not abuse Jesus Christ, and speak ill of him? And what am I in comparison of Christ? And the subjection of Christ to such an evil was for me, that though such a thing should come upon me, I might know that the curse of it is taken from me through Christ's subjection to that evil. Thus, a Christian can be content when anybody speaks ill of him. Now, this is a mystery to you, to get contentment in this way. So if men jeer and scoff at you, did they not do so to Jesus Christ? They jeered and scoffed at him, and that when he was in his greatest extremity upon the Cross: they said, Here is the King of the Jews, and they bowed the knee, and said, Hail King of the Jews, and put a reed into his hand, and mocked him. Now I get contentment in the midst of scorns and jeers, by considering that Christ was scorned, and by acting faith upon what Christ suffered for me. Am I in great bodily pain? – Jesus Christ had as great pain in his body as I have (though it is true he did not have the same kind of sicknesses as we have, yet he had as great pain and tortures in his body, and that which was deadly to him, as much as any sickness is to us). The exercising of faith on what Christ endured, is the way to get contentment in the midst of our pains. Someone lies vexing and fretting himself, and cannot bear his pain: are you a Christian? Have you ever tried this way of getting contentment, to act your faith on all the pains and sufferings that Jesus Christ suffered: this would be the way of contentment, and a Christian gets contentment when under pains, in this way. Sometimes one who is very godly and gracious, may be found bearing grievous pains and extremities very cheerfully, and you wonder at it. He gets it by acting his faith upon what pains Jesus Christ suffered. You are afraid of death – the way to get contentment is by exercising your faith on the death of Jesus Christ. It may be that you have inward troubles in your soul, and God withdraws himself from you; still your faith is to be exercised upon the sufferings that Jesus Christ endured in his soul. He poured forth his soul before God, and when he sweat drops of water and blood, he was in an agony in his very spirit, and he found even God himself about to forsake him. Now thus to act your faith on Jesus Christ brings contentment, and is not this a mystery to carnal hearts? A gracious heart finds contentment as a mystery; it is no marvel that St Paul said, 'I am instructed in a mystery, to be contented in whatsoever condition I am in.'

XI. There is still a further mystery, for I hope you will find this a very useful point and that before we have finished you will see how simple it is for one who is skilled in religion to get contentment, though it is hard for one who is carnal. I say,

[62]

the eleventh mystery in contentment is this: *A gracious heart has contentment by getting strength from Jesus Christ; he is able to bear his burden by getting strength from someone else.* Now this is a riddle, and it would be counted ridiculous in the schools of the philosophers, to say, If there is a burden on you you must get strength from someone else. Indeed if you must have another come and stand under the burden, they could understand that; but that you should be strengthened by the strength of someone else, who is not near you as far as you can see, they would think that ridiculous. But a Christian finds satisfaction in every circumstance by getting strength from another, by going out of himself to Jesus Christ, by his faith acting upon Christ, and bringing the strength of Jesus Christ into his own soul, he is thereby enabled to bear whatever God lays on him, by the strength that he finds from Jesus Christ. Of his fullness do we receive grace for grace; there is strength in Christ not only to sanctify and save us, but strength to support us under all our burdens and afflictions, and Christ expects that when we are under any burden, we should act our faith upon him to draw virtue and strength from him. Faith is the great grace that is to be acted under afflictions. It is true that other graces should be acted, but the grace of faith draws strength from Christ, in looking on him who has the fullness of all strength conveyed into the hearts of all believers.

Now if a man has a burden to bear, and yet can have strength added to him – if the burden is doubled, he can have his strength trebled – the burden will not be heavier but lighter than it was before to his natural strength. Indeed, our afflictions may be heavy, and we cry out, Oh, we cannot bear them, we cannot bear such an affliction. Though you cannot tell how to bear it with your own strength, yet how can you tell what you will do with the strength of Jesus Christ? You say you cannot bear it? So you think that Christ could not bear it? But if Christ could bear it why may you not come to bear it? You will say, Can I have the strength of Christ? Yes, it is made over to you by faith: the Scripture says that the Lord is our strength, God himself is our strength, and Christ is our strength. There are many Scriptures to that effect, that Christ's strength is yours, made over to you, so that you may be able to bear whatever lies upon you, and therefore we find such a strange expression in the Epistle of St Paul to the Colossians, praying for the saints: 'That they might be strengthened with all might according unto his glorious power', unto what? 'Unto all patience and longsuffering with joyfulness' – strengthened with all might, according to the power of God, the glorious power of God, unto all patience, and longsuffering with joyfulness. You must not therefore be content with a little strength, so that you are able to bear what a man might bear by the strength of reason and nature, but you should be strengthened with all might, according to the glorious power of God, unto all patience, and to all longsuffering.

Oh, you who are now under very heavy and sad afflictions more than usual, look at this Scripture, and consider how it is made good in you; and why may you not have this Scripture made good in you, if you are godly? You should not be quiet in your own spirits, unless in some measure you get this Scripture made good in you, so that you may with some comfort say, 'Through God's mercy, I find that strength coming into me that is spoken of in this Scripture.' You should labour when you are under any great affliction (you who are godly) to walk so that others may see such a Scripture made good in you. This is the glorious power of God that strengthens his servants to all longsuffering, and that with joyfulness. Alas, it may be that you do not exercise as much patience as a wise man or a wise woman who has only natural reason. But where is the power of God, the glorious power of God? Where is the strengthening with all might, unto all longsuffering and patience, and that with joyfulness? It is true, the spirit of a man may be able to sustain his infirmities, may be able to sustain and keep up his spirits, the natural spirit of a man can do that, but much more when the spirit is endued with grace and holiness, and when it is filled with the strength of Jesus Christ. This is the way a godly man gets contentment, the mystery of it, by getting strength from Jesus Christ.

[64]

XII. *A godly heart enjoys much of God in everything he has, and knows how to make up all wants in God himself.* That is another mystery, he has God in what he has. I spoke about that somewhat before, in showing the dew of God's blessing in what one has, for God is able to let out a great deal of his power in little things, and therefore the miracles that God has wrought, have been as much in little things as in great. Now just as God lets out a great deal of his power in working miracles in smaller things, so he lets out a great deal of goodness and mercy, in comforting and rejoicing the hearts of his people in little things, as well as in great. There may be as great riches in a pearl as in a great deal of lumber; but this is a different thing.

Further, just as a gracious heart lives upon God's dew in the little that he has, so when the little that he has shall be taken from him, what shall he do then? Then, you will say, If a man has nothing, nothing can be got out of nothing. But if the children of God have their little taken from them, they can make up all their wants in God himself. Such and such a man is a poor man, the plunderers came and took away everything that he had; what shall he do now that all is gone? But when all is gone, there is an art and skill that godliness teaches, to make up all those losses in God. Many men whose houses have been burnt go about gathering, and so get together by many hands a little; but a godly man knows where to go, to get up all, even in God himself, so that he may enjoy the quintessence of the same good and comfort as he had before, for a godly man does not live so much in himself as he lives in God. Now this is a mystery to a carnal heart. I say a gracious man does not live so much in himself as in God; he lives in God continually. If anything is cut off from the stream, he knows how to go to the fountain, and makes up all there. God is his all in all, while he lives; I say it is God who is his all in all. 'Am not I to thee', said Elkanah to Hannah, 'instead of ten children?' So says God to a gracious heart: 'You lack this, your estate is plundered – Why? Am not I to you instead of ten homes, and ten shops, I am to you instead of all; and not only instead of all, but come to me, and you shall have all again in me.'

This indeed is an excellent art, to be able to draw from God what one had before in the creature. Christian, how did you enjoy comfort before? Was the creature anything to you but a conduit, a pipe, that conveyed God's goodness to you? 'The pipe is cut off,' says God, 'come to me, the fountain, and drink immediately.' Though the beams are taken away, yet the sun remains the same in the firmament as ever it was. What is it that satisfies God himself, but that he enjoys all fullness in himself; so he comes to have satisfaction in himself. Now if you enjoy God as your portion, if your soul can say with the Church in Lamentations 3. 24: 'The Lord is my portion, saith my soul', why should you not be satisfied and contented like God? God is contented, he is in eternal contentment in himself; now if you have that God as your portion, why should you not be contented with him alone? Since God is contented with himself alone, if you have him, you may be contented with him alone, and it may be, that is the reason why your outward comforts are taken from you, that God may be all in all to you. It may be that while you had these things they shared with God in your affection, a great part of the stream of your affection ran that way; God would have the full stream run to him now. You know when a man has water coming to his house, through several pipes, and he finds insufficient water comes into his wash-house, he will rather stop the other pipes that he may have all the water come in where he wants it. Perhaps, then, God had a stream of your affection running to him when you enjoyed these things; yes, but a great deal was allowed to escape to the creature, a great deal of your affections ran waste. Now the Lord would not have the affections of his children to run waste; he does not care for other men's affections, but yours are precious, and God would not have them to run waste; therefore he has cut off your other pipes that your heart might flow wholly to him. If you have children, and because you let your servants perhaps feed them and give them things, you perceive that your servants are stealing away the hearts of your children, you would hardly be able to bear it; you would be ready to send away such a servant. When the servant is gone, the child is at a great loss, it has not got the nurse, but the father or mother intends by sending her away, that the affections of the child might run more strongly towards himself or herself, and what loss is it to the child that the affections that ran in a rough channel before towards the servant, run now towards the mother? So those affections that run towards the creature, God would have run towards himself, that so he may be all in all to you here in this world.

A gracious heart can indeed tell how to enjoy God as all in all to him. That is the happiness of heaven to have God to be all in all. The saints in heaven do not have houses, and lands, and money, and meat and drink, and clothes; you will say, they do not need them – why not? It is because God is all in all to them immediately. Now while you live in this world, you may come to enjoy much of God, you may have much of heaven, while we live in this life we may come to enjoy much of the very life that is in heaven, and what is that but the enjoyment of God to be all in all to us? There is one text in the Revelation that speaks of the glorious condition of the Church that is likely to be here even in this world: 'And I saw no temple therein, for the Lord God Almighty and the Lamb are the temple of it, and the city had no need of the sun, neither of the moon to shine in it, for the glory of God did lighten it, and the Lamb is the light thereof' (Revelation 21. 22). They had no need of the sun or moon. It speaks of such a glorious condition that the Church is likely to be in here in this world; this does not speak of heaven, but of a glorious estate that the Church shall be in here, in this world; and that appears plainly, for it follows immediately in the 24th and 26th verses, 'And the Kings of the earth do bring their glory and honour into it'; why, the Kings of the earth shall not bring their glory and honour into heaven, but this is such a time, when the Kings of the earth shall bring their glory and honour to the Church. And in the 26th verse, 'And they shall bring the glory and honour of the nations into it'; therefore here it must mean this world and not heaven. Now if there is to be such a time here in this world, when God shall be all in all, and in comparison there shall be no such need of creatures as there is now, then the saints should labour to live as near that life as possibly they can, that is, to make up all in God.

Oh, that you would consider this mystery, that it may be a reality to the hearts of the saints in such times as these. They would find this privilege that they get by grace worth thousands of worlds. Hence is that statement of Jacob's that I have mentioned in another case; it is remarkable, and is very pertinent here. In that remarkable speech of Jacob, in Genesis 33, when his brother Esau met him, you find in one place that Esau refused Jacob's present; in the 8th verse, when Jacob gave his present to him, he refused it, and told Jacob that he had enough: 'What meanest thou by all this drove which I met? And he said, these are to find grace in thy sight: And Esau said, I have enough.' Now in the 11th verse Jacob urges it still, and, says Jacob, 'I beseech thee, take it, for I have enough.' Now in your Bibles it is the same in English – I have enough, saith Esau, and, I have enough, saith Jacob – but in the Hebrew Jacob's word is different from Esau's: Jacob's word signifies *I have all things*, and yet Jacob was poorer than Esau. Oh, this should be a shame to us that an Esau can say, I have enough. But a Christian should say, I have not only enough, but I have all. How did he have all? – because he had God who was all. It was a remarkable saying of one, 'He has all things who has him that has all things'. Surely you have all things, because you have him for your portion who has all things: God has all things in himself, and you have God for your portion, and in that you have all, and this is the mystery of contentment. It makes up all its wants in God: this is what the men of the world have little skill in.

Now I have many other things still to open in the mystery of contentment. I should show likewise that a godly man not only makes up everything in God, but finds enough in himself to make up all – to make up everything in himself, not from

[68]

himself, but in himself – and that may seem to be stranger than the other. To make up everything in God is something, nay, to make up everything in himself (not from himself but in himself) – a gracious heart has so much of God within himself, that he has enough there to make up all his outward wants. In Proverbs 14. 14 we read, 'A good man shall be satisfied from himself', from that which is within himself – that is the meaning. A gracious man has a bird within his own bosom which makes him melody enough, though he lacks music. 'The Kingdom of heaven is within you' (Luke 17. 21). He has a Kingdom within him, a Kingdom of God; you see him spoken ill of abroad, but he has a conscience within him that makes up the want of a name and credit, that is instead of a thousand witnesses.

XIII. *A gracious heart gets contentment from the Covenant that God has made with him.* Now this is a way of getting contentment that the men of the world do not know : they can get contentment, if they have the creature to satisfy them; but in getting contentment from the Covenant of grace they have little skill. I should have opened two things here, first, how to get contentment from the Covenant of grace in general (but I shall speak of that in the next sermon, and now, only a word on the second). Secondly, how he gets contentment from the particular branches of the Covenant, that is, from the particular promises that he has, for supplying every particular want. There is no condition that a godly man or woman can be in, but there is some promise or other in the Scripture to help him in that condition. And that is the way of his contentment, to go to the promises, and get from the promise, that which may supply. This is but a dry business to a carnal heart; but it is the most real thing in the world to a gracious heart : when he finds lack of contentment he repairs to the promise, and the Covenant, and falls to pleading the promises that God has made. As I should have shown several promises that God has made, whatever the affliction, I will only mention one, that is, the saddest affliction of all, in case of the visitation, and the plague (Psalm 91). Those whose friends cannot come to them by reason of the plague, and who cannot have other comforts, in other afflictions might have their friends and other things to comfort them – but in that they cannot. We read, 'There shall no evil befall thee, neither shall any plague come nigh thy dwelling'; then there is a promise for the pestilence in the 5th and 6th verses, this is a Scripture to those who are in danger of it. You will say that this is a promise that the plague shall not come nigh them; but mark that these two are joined: there shall no evil befall thee, neither shall the plague come nigh thee, the evil of it shall not come nigh thee.

Objection: You will say, but it does come to many godly men, and how can they make use of this Scripture? It is rather a Scripture that may trouble them, because here is a promise that it shall not come nigh them, and yet it does come nigh them as well as others.

Answer: 1. The promises of outward deliverance that were made to the people of God in the time of the law, were to be understood then a great deal more literally, and fulfilled more literally, than in the times of the gospel when God makes it up otherwise with as much mercy. Though God made a Covenant of grace and eternal life in Christ with them, yet I think there was another covenant too, which God speaks of as a distinct covenant for outward things, to deal with his people according to their ways, either in outward prosperity, or in outward afflictions, more so than now, in a more punctual, set way, than in the times of the gospel. Therefore when the children of Israel sinned against God, they were sure to have public judgments come upon them, and if they did well, always public mercies; the general, constant way of God was to deal with the people of the Jews according as they did well or ill, with outward judgments and outward mercies. But it is not so now in the times of the gospel; we cannot bring such a certain conclusion, that if God did deal so severely with men by such and such afflictions, he will deal so with them now, or that they shall have outward prosperity as they had then. Therefore, that is the first thing, for understanding this and all other texts of the kind.

[70]

2. Perhaps their faith does not attain to this promise; and God often brings many outward afflictions, because the faith of his people does not reach the promise, and that not only in the Old Testament, but in the times of the New Testament. Zacharias' time may be said to be in the time of the New Testament, when he was struck with dumbness because he did not believe; and that is given as the cause why he was struck with dumbness. But you will say now, has faith a warrant to believe deliverance, that it shall be fully delivered? I dare not say so, but it may act upon it, to believe that God will make it good in his own way. Perhaps you have not done as much, and so because of that, this promise is not fulfilled to you.

3. When God makes such a promise to his people, yet still it must be with this reservation, that God must have liberty for these three things.

i. That notwithstanding his promise, he will have liberty to make use of anything for your chastisement.

ii. That he must have liberty, to make use of your wealth, or liberties, or lives, for the furtherance of his own ends, if it is to be a stumbling block to wicked and ungodly men. God must have liberty, though he has made a promise to you he will not release the propriety that he has in your possessions and lives.

iii. God must have sufficient liberty to make use of what you have, to show that his ways are unsearchable, and his judgments past finding out. God reserves these three things in his hand still.

Objection: But you will say, What good then is there in such a promise that God makes to his people?

1. That you are under the protection of God more than others. But what comfort is this if it befalls me?

Answer: You have this comfort, that the evil of it shall be taken from you, that if God will make use of this affliction for other ends, yet he will do it so as to make it up to you in some other way. Perhaps you have given your children something, but afterwards if you have a use for that thing, you will come and say, 'I must have it'. 'Why, father?' the child may say, 'you gave it me.' 'But I must have it', says the father, 'and I will make it up to you in some other way.' The child does not think that the father's love is ever a whit the less to him. So when there is any such promise as this, that God by his promise gives you his protection, and yet for all that, such a thing befalls you, it is only as if the father should say, 'I gave you that indeed, but let me have it and I will make it up to you in some other way that shall be as good.' God says, 'Let me have your health and liberty, and life, and it shall be made up to you in some other way.'

2. Whenever the plague or pestilence comes to those who are under such a promise, it is for some special and notable work, and God requires them to search and examine in a special manner, to find out his meaning; there is so much to be learned in the promise that God has made concerning this particular evil, that the people of God may come to quiet and content their hearts in this affliction. I read in this Psalm that God has made a promise to his people, to deliver them from the plague and pestilence, and yet I find it has come. It may be that I have not made use of my faith in this promise heretofore; and if God brings afflictions upon me, yet he will make it up some other way. God made a promise to deliver me, or at least to deliver me from all the evil of it; now if this thing does befall me and yet I have a promise of God, certainly the evil of it is taken away. This promise tells me that if it does befall me yet it is for some notable end, and because God has a use for my life, and intends to bring about his glory some way that I do not know of. And if he will come in a fatherly way of chastisement, yet I will be satisfied in the thing. So a Christian heart, by reasoning out of the Word, comes to satisfy his soul in the midst of such a heavy hand of God, and in such a distressed condition as that. Now carnal hearts do not find that power in the Word, that healing virtue that is in it, to heal their distracting cares, and the troubles of their spirits; but when those who are godly come to hear the Word, they find in it, as it were, a plaster for all their wounds, and so they come to have ease and contentment in such conditions as are

very grievous and miserable to others. But as for other particular promises, and more generally for the Covenant of grace, how and in what a mysterious way the saints work to get contentment and satisfaction to their souls, we shall refer to these things in the next chapter.

4

THE MYSTERY OF CONTENTMENT – *concluded*

In the last chapter we spoke of several things in the mystery of contentment, and at the close we spoke of two more, but we did not have time to open either of them. I shall now open them a little more fully, then proceed to some few more.

That is the next thing then: a Christian heart not only has contentment in God, and certainly he who has God (who himself has all) must have all, but *he is able to make up all his outward wants of creature comforts from what he finds in himself*. That may seem to be more strange. It is true, perhaps, that even though men do not feel by experience what it is to make up all in God, yet we may convince them that if they have him who has all things then they have all, for there is such a fullness in God, he being the infinite first being of all things, that may make up all their wants. But here is another thing, that is beyond that; I say a godly man can make up whatever he lacks without the creature, he can make it up in himself. In Proverbs 14. 14 we read: 'A good man shall be satisfied from himself.' Suppose for example, that he lacks outward comforts, good cheer and feasting, a good conscience is a continual feast; so he can make up the lack of a feast by the peace that he has in his own conscience. If he lacks melody in the world, he has a bird within him that sings the most melodious songs in the world, and the most delightful. And then does he lack honour? He has his own conscience witnessing for him, that is as a thousand witnesses. The Scripture says (in Luke 17. 21): 'Neither shall they say, Lo here! or, Lo there! for behold the kingdom of God is within you.' A Christian, then, whatever he lacks he can make it up, for he has a kingdom in himself: 'the kingdom of God is within you'.

If a king meets with a great deal of trouble when he is abroad, he contents himself with this: 'I have a Kingdom of my own.' It is said here, the Kingdom of God is within a man; now if those of you who are learned look into the Commentary on this Gospel by a certain scholar, you will find he has a very strange idea about this text: he confesses that it is unutterable and so it is, the kingdom of God is within you, but he understands it that there is such a presence of God and Christ within the soul of a man, that when the body dies, he says, the soul goes into God and Christ who are within him. The soul's going into God and Christ, and enjoying that communion with God and Christ that is within itself, that is Heaven to it, he says. He confesses he is not able to express himself, and others cannot understand fully what he means; but certainly for the present, before death, there is a Kingdom of God within the soul, such a manifestation of God in the soul as is enough to content the heart of any godly man in the world, the Kingdom that he now has within him. He need not wait till afterwards, till he goes to Heaven; but certainly there is a Heaven in the soul of a godly man, he has Heaven already. Many times when you go to comfort your friends in their afflictions, you say, 'Heaven will pay for all'; indeed, you may assuredly find Heaven pays for all already. There is a Heaven within the souls of the saints – that is a certain truth; no soul shall ever come to Heaven, but the soul which has Heaven come to it first. When you die, you hope you will go to Heaven; but if you will go to Heaven when you die, Heaven will come to you before you die.

Now this is a great mystery, to have the Kingdom of Heaven in the soul; no man can know this but that soul which has it. The Heaven which is within the soul for the present is like the white stone and the new name, that none but those that have it can understand it. It is a miserable condition, my brethren, to depend altogether upon creatures for our contentment. You know that rich men account it a great happiness, if they do not need to go to buy things by the penny as others do; they have all things for pleasure or profit on their own ground, and all their inheritance lies entire together, nobody comes within them, but they have everything within themselves: there lies their happiness. Whereas other, poorer people are fain to go from one market to another to provide their necessities, great rich men have sheep and beeves, corn and clothing, and all things else of their own within themselves, and herein they place their happiness. But this is the happiness of a Christian, that he has that within himself which may satisfy him more than all these. There is a place in the first chapter of James that seems to allude to the condition of men who have all their wealth within themselves: 'But let patience have her perfect work that ye may be perfect, and entire, wanting nothing' (James 1. 4). The word there used signifies to have the whole inheritance to ourselves, not a broken inheritance, but that where all lies within themselves, not like a man who has a piece of his estate here, and a piece there, but one who has it all lying together. When the heart is patient under afflictions it finds itself in such an estate as this, finds its whole inheritance together, and all complete within itself.

Now to show this by further analogies: the one who is filled with good things is just like many a man who enjoys an abundance of comforts at home, in his own house. God grants him a pleasant home, a good wife, and fine walks and gardens, and he has all things at home that he could desire. Now such a man does not care much for going out. Other men are fain to go out and see friends, because they have quarrelling and contending at home. Many poor husbands will give this reason, if their wives moan, and complain of their faults and short-comings. They make it their excuse to go out, because they can never be quiet at home. Now we account those men most happy who have everything at home. Those who have con-fined homes that are unpleasant and evil-smelling delight to go into the fresh air, but it is not so with many others that have good things at home. Those who have no good cheer at home are fain to go out to friends, but those whose tables are well furnished would as soon stay at home. So a carnal man has little contentment in his own spirit. It is Augustine who likens a bad conscience to a scolding wife: a man who has a bad conscience does not care to look into his own soul, but loves to be out, and to look into other things; he never looks to himself. But one who has a good conscience delights in looking into his own heart; he has a good conscience within him. A carnal heart seeks his contentment elsewhere because there is nothing but a filthy stink, vileness and baseness within himself.

As it is with a vessel that is full of liquor, if you strike it, it will make no great noise, but if it is empty then it makes a great noise; so it is with the heart, a heart that is full of grace and goodness within will bear a great many strokes, and never make any noise, but if an empty heart is struck it will make a noise. When some men and women are complaining so much, and always whining, it is a sign that there is an emptiness in their hearts. If their hearts were filled with grace they would not make such a noise. A man whose bones are filled with marrow, and his veins with good blood does not complain of the cold as others do. So a gracious heart, having the Spirit of God within him, and his heart filled with grace has that within him that makes him find contentment. It was a saying of Seneca: 'Those things that I suffer will be incredibly heavy when I cannot bear myself.' But if I am no burden to myself, if all is quiet within my own heart, then I can bear anything. Many men through their wickedness have burdens outside, but the greatest burden is the wickedness of their own hearts. They are not burdened with their sins in a godly way, for that would ease their burden, but they still have their wickedness in its power, and so they are burdens to themselves. The disorders of men's hearts are great burdens to them, but many times a godly man has enough within to content him. Virtue is content with itself, to live well – it is a saying of Cicero, in one of his Paradoxes – it finds enough within its own sphere for living happily. But how few are acquainted with this mystery! Many think, O if I had what another man has, how happily and comfortably should I live! But if you are a Christian, whatever your condition, you have enough within yourself. You will say, such and such men who have all things need not be beholden to anybody. There are many who labour and take pains when they are young, that they might not be beholden to others; they love to live of themselves. Now a Christian may do so, not that he does not live upon God (I do not mean that), but upon what he has of God within himself: he can live upon that, although he does not enjoy the comforts that are outside himself. That is what I mean, and those who are godly and keep close to God in their communion with him will understand what I mean by saying that a Christian has the supply of all his wants within himself. Here you may see that the spirit of a Christian is a precious spirit; a godly spirit is precious, why? Because it has enough to make him happy within himself.

The next thing that the mystery of contentment consists in is this, *That a gracious heart gets its supply of all things from the Covenant, and so comes to have contentment*, which is a dry thing to a carnal spirit.

There are two things in this:

1. He gets contentment from the Covenant *in general*, that is, from the great covenant that God has made with him in Christ.

2. He gets it from the *particular promises* that God has made with him in the Covenant.

1. *From the Covenant in general*. I will give you one Scripture for that, which is very striking: 'Although my house be not so with God, yet he hath made with me an everlasting covenant, ordered in all things, and sure: for this is all my salvation, and all my desire, although he make it not to grow' (2 Samuel 23. 5). It is a wonderful statement by David, who did not have the Covenant of Grace revealed as fully as we have. Mark what he says: 'Although I find not my house so', that is, so comfortable in every way as I would wish, although it is not so, what has he got to content his spirit? He

says, 'He has made with me an everlasting covenant,' this is what helps in everything. Some men will say, I am not thus and thus with God, I do not find that God comes in so fully, or it is not with my house and family as I hoped it might be, perhaps there is this or that affliction upon my house. Suppose the plague were to come into your house, and it is not so safe, and you do not enjoy such outward comfort in your house as you once did. Can you read this Scripture and say, Although my house is not so blessed with health as other men's houses are, although my house is not so, yet he has made with me an everlasting covenant. I am still one in covenant with God, the Lord has made with me an everlasting covenant. As for these things in the world, I see they are but momentary, they are not everlasting. I see a family in which all was well only a week ago, and now everything is down, the plague has swept away a great many of them, and the rest are left in sadness and mourning. We see there is no resting in the things of this world, yet the Lord has made with me an everlasting covenant ordered in all things. I find disorder in my heart, in my family; but the everlasting covenant is ordered in all things, yes, and it is sure.

Alas, there is no certainty here in these things. We can be sure of nothing here, especially in these times; we know that a man can be sure of little that he has, and who can be sure of his wealth? Perhaps some of you here have lived well and comfortably before, all was well about you, and you thought your mountain was strong, but within a day or two you see everything taken away from you – there is no certainty in the things of this world; but he says, the Covenant is sure. What I venture at sea is not sure, but here is an insurance office indeed, a great insurance office for the saints, at which they are not charged, except in the exercising of grace, for they may go to this insurance office to insure everything that they venture, either to have the thing itself, or to be paid for it. In an insurance office you cannot be sure to have the very goods that you insured, but if they are lost the insurers pledge themselves to make it good to you. And this

Covenant of grace that God has made with his people is God's insurance office, and the saints in all their fears may and ought to go to the Covenant to insure all things, to insure their wealth and insure their lives. You will say, How are they sure? Their lives and wealth go as well as other people's do. But God pledges himself to make up all. And mark what follows, 'This is all my salvation' – Why, David, will you not have salvation from your enemies and from outward dangers, pestilence and plague? The frame of his spirit is quieted, as though to say: if that salvation comes, well and good, I shall praise God for it; but what I have in the Covenant, that is my salvation, I look upon that as enough. Yes, and he goes further, 'This is all my salvation and all my desire' – Why, David, is there not something else that you would like to have besides this Covenant? No, he says, it is all involved in this. Surely, those men or women must needs live contented lives who have all their desires? Now, says the holy man here, this is all my desire, though he make it not to grow. For all this Covenant, perhaps, you will not prosper in the world as other men do, true; but I can bear that. Though God does not make my house to grow, I have all my desires.

Thus you see how a godly heart finds contentment in the Covenant. Many of you speak of the Covenant of God, and of the Covenant of grace; but have you found it as effectual as this to your souls, have you sucked this sweetness from the Covenant, and contentment to your hearts in your sad conditions. It is a special sign of true grace in any soul, that when any affliction befalls him, in a kind of natural way he repairs immediately to the Covenant. Just as a child, as soon as ever it is in danger, need not be told to go to his father or mother, for nature tells him so; so it is with a gracious heart: as soon as it is in any trouble or affliction there is a new nature which carries him to the Covenant immediately, where he finds ease and rest. If you find that your hearts work in this way, immediately running to the Covenant, it is an excellent sign of true grace: so much for the general point.

2. But now for *particular promises* in the Covenant of

grace. A gracious heart looks upon every promise as coming from the root of the great Covenant, of grace in Christ. Other men look upon some particular promises, that God will help them in straits, and keep them and the like, but they do not look at the connection of such particular promises, to the root, the Covenant of grace. Christians miss a great deal of comfort which they might have from the particular promises in the gospel, if they would consider their connection to the root, the great Covenant that God has made with them in Christ. In the times of the law, they might rest more upon outward promises than we can in the time of the gospel. I gave you the reason why we who live in the times of the gospel cannot depend so much on a literal fulfilment of the outward promises that we find in the Old Testament, as they could in the time of the law. For there was a special covenant, that God pleased to call a New Covenant, by way of distinction from the other covenant, that is made with us in Christ for eternal life. So even the law was given to them in a more peculiar way for an external covenant of outward blessings in the land of Canaan, and so God dealt with them in a more external covenant than he does now with his people. Yet godliness has the promise of this life, and that which is to come. We may make use of the promises for this life, but yet not so much to rest upon the literal performance of them as they of old might. But God will make them good in some way or other, in a spiritual way if not in an outward way. We must lay no more upon outward promises than this, and therefore if we lay more, we make the promise to bear more than it will bear.

To give some examples: to believe fully and confidently, that the plague shall not come nigh a certain house, is, I say, to lay more upon such a promise than it will bear. If you remember, I opened that promise in Psalm 91. Now if I had lived in the time of the law, perhaps I might have been somewhat more confident of the literal performance of the promise, than I can be now in the time of the gospel. The promise now bears no more than this, that God has a special protection over his people, and that he will deliver them from the evil of such an affliction, and if he does bring such an affliction, it is more than an ordinary providence, it is a special providence that God has in it. I thought I would give you several promises for the contentment of the heart in the time of affliction: 'When thou passest through the waters I will be with thee, and through the rivers, they shall not overflow thee; when thou walkest through the fire thou shalt not be burnt, neither shall the flame kindle upon thee' (Isaiah 43: 2). Certainly, though this promise was made in the time of the law, it will be made good to all the saints now, one way or other, either literally or in some other way. For we find clearly that the promise that was made to Joshua, 'I will not fail thee nor forsake thee' (Joshua 1. 5) is applied to Christians in the time of the Gospel.

So here is the way of faith in bringing contentment by the promises: the saints of God have an interest in all the promises that ever were made to our forefathers, from the beginning of the world they are their inheritance, and go on from one generation to another. By that they come to have contentment, because they inherit all the promises made in all the book of God. Hebrews 13. 5 shows this plainly, that it is our inheritance, and we do not inherit less now than they did in Joshua's time, but we inherit more. For you will find in that place of Hebrews that more is said than is to Joshua. To Joshua God says, He will not leave him nor forsake him; but in this place in Hebrews in the Greek there are five negatives, I will not, not, not, not, not again. That is the force of it in the Greek. I say, there are five negatives in that little sentence; as if God should say, I will not leave you, no I will not, I will not, I will not, with such earnestness five times together. So that not only have we the same promises that they had, but we have them more enlarged and more full, though still not so much in the literal sense, for that, indeed, is the least part of the promise. In Isaiah 54. 17 God made a promise: That no weapon formed against his people should prosper, and every tongue that shall rise against them in judgment they shall condemn, and mark what follows, 'This is the heritage of the servants of the Lord, and their righteousness is of me, saith the Lord.' This is a good promise for a soldier, though still we ought not to lay too much upon the literal sense. True, it holds forth thus much, that God's protection is in a special manner over the soldiers that are godly. 'And every tongue that shall rise against thee in judgment thou shalt condemn' – this is against false witness too. Oh you, whose friends never left you anything! you will say, My friends died and did not leave me a groat; but I thank God, he has provided for me. Though your father or mother died and left you no inheritance, you have an inheritance in the promise, 'This is their heritage.' So that there is no godly man or woman, but is a great heir.

Therefore when you look into the book of God and find any promise there, you may make it your own; just as an heir who rides over a lot of fields and meadows says, This meadow is my inheritance, and this corn field is my inheritance, and then he sees a fine house, and says, This fine house is my inheritance. He looks at them with a different eye from a stranger who rides over those fields. A carnal heart reads the promises, and reads them merely as stories, not that he has any great interest in them. But every time a godly man reads the Scriptures (remember this when you are reading the Scripture) and there meets with a promise, he ought to lay his hand upon it and say, This is part of my inheritance, it is mine, and I am to live upon it. This will make you contented; it is a mysterious way of getting contentment. And there are several other promises that bring contentment (Psalms 34. 10, 37. 6; Isaiah 58. 10). So much for the mystery of contentment by way of the Covenant.

There are two or three things more that show how a godly man has contentment in a mysterious way different from any carnal heart in the world, as follows:

XIV. *He has contentment by realizing the glorious things of Heaven to him.* He has the kingdom of Heaven as present, and the glory that is to come; by faith he makes it present. So the martyrs had contentment in their sufferings, for some of them said, 'Though we have but a hard breakfast, yet we shall have a good dinner, we shall very soon be in heaven.' 'Do but

shut your eyes', said one, 'and you shall be in heaven at once.'
'We faint not', says the Apostle (2 Corinthians 4. 16). Why?
Because these light afflictions that are but for a moment, work
for us a far more exceeding and eternal weight of glory.
They see heaven before them and that contents them. When
you sailors see the haven before you, though you were
mightily troubled before you could see any land, yet when
you come near the shore and can see a certain land-mark,
that contents you greatly. A godly man in the midst of the
waves and storms that he meets with can see the glory of
heaven before him and so contents himself. One drop of the
sweetness of heaven is enough to take away all the sourness
and bitterness of all the afflictions in the world. We know
that one drop of sourness, or one drop of gall will make bitter
a great deal of honey. Put a spoonful of sugar into a cup of
gall or wormwood, and it will not sweeten it; but if you put a
spoonful of gall into a cup of sugar, it will embitter that. Now
it is otherwise in heaven : one drop of sweetness will sweeten
a great deal of sour affliction, but a great deal of sourness and
gall will not embitter a soul who sees the glory of heaven that
is to come. A carnal heart has no contentment but from what
he sees before him in this world, but a godly heart has contentment from what he sees laid up for him in the highest
heavens.

XV. The last thing that I would mention is this, *A godly
man has contentment by opening and letting out his heart to
God*. Other men or women are discontented, but how do they
help themselves? By abuse, by bad language. Someone crosses
them, and they have no way to help themselves but by abuse
and by bitter words, and so they relieve themselves in that
way when they are angry. But when a godly man is crossed,
how does he relieve himself? – He is aware of his cross as well
as you, but he goes to God in prayer, and there opens his
heart to God and lets out his sorrows and fears, and then can
come away with a joyful countenance. Do you find that you
can come away from prayer and not look sad? It is said of
Hannah, that when she had been at prayer her countenance

was no more sad (1 Samuel 1. 18), she was comforted: this is the right way to contentment.

Thus we have done with the mystery of contentment. Now if you can but put these things together that we have spoken of, you may see fully what an art Christian contentment is.

5

HOW CHRIST TEACHES CONTENTMENT

Contentment is not such a poor business as many make it. They say, 'You must be content', and so on. But Paul needed to learn it, and it is a great art and mystery of godliness to be content in a Christian way, and it will be seen to be even more of a mystery when we come to show what lessons a gracious heart learns when it learns to be contented. I have learned to be contented; what lessons have you learned? Take a scholar who has great learning and understanding in arts and sciences; how did he begin? He began, as we say, his ABC, and then afterwards he came to his Testament, and Bible and accidence,* and so to his grammar, and afterwards to his other books; so he learned one thing after another. So a Christian coming to contentment is as a scholar in Christ's school, and there are many lessons to teach the soul to bring it to this learning; every godly man or woman is a scholar. It cannot be said of any Christian that he is illiterate, but he is literate, a learned man, a learned woman. Now the lessons that Christ teaches to bring us to contentment are these:

I. *The lesson of self-denial*. It is a hard lesson. You know that when a child is first taught, he complains: This is hard; it is just like that. I remember Bradford the martyr said, 'Whoever has not learned the lesson of the cross, has not learned his ABC in Christianity.' This is where Christ begins with his scholars, and those in the lowest form must begin with this; if you mean to be Christians at all, you must buckle to this or

* Accidence = the part of grammar dealing with inflexions.

you can never be Christians. Just as no-one can be a scholar unless he learns his ABC, so you must learn the lesson of self-denial or you can never become a scholar in Christ's school, and be learned in this mystery of contentment. That is the first lesson that Christ teaches any soul, self-denial, which brings contentment, which brings down and softens a man's heart. You know how when you strike something soft it makes no noise, but if you strike a hard thing it makes a noise; so with the hearts of men who are full of themselves, and hardened with self-love, if they receive a stroke they make a noise, but a self-denying Christian yields to God's hand, and makes no noise. When you strike a woolsack it makes no noise because it yields to the stroke; so a self-denying heart yields to the stroke and thereby comes to this contentment. Now there are several things in this lesson of self-denial. I will not enter into the doctrine of self-denial, but only show you how Christ teaches self-denial and how that brings contentment.

1. *Such a person learns to know that he is nothing.* He comes to this, to be able to say, 'Well, I see I am nothing in myself.' That man or woman who indeed knows that he or she is nothing, and has learned it thoroughly will be able to bear anything. The way to be able to bear anything is to know that we are nothing in ourselves. God says to us, 'Wilt thou set thine eyes upon that which is not' (Proverbs 23. 5) speaking of riches. Why, blessed God, do not you do so? you have set your heart upon us and yet we are nothing. God would not have us set our hearts upon riches, because they are nothing, and yet God is pleased to set his heart upon us, and we are nothing: that is God's grace, free grace, and therefore it does not much matter what I suffer, for I am as nothing.

2. *I deserve nothing.* I am nothing, and I deserve nothing. Suppose I lack this and that thing which others have? I am sure that I deserve nothing except it be Hell. You will answer any of your servants, who is not content: I wonder what you think you deserve? or your children: do you deserve it that you are so eager to have it? You would stop their mouths thus, and so we may easily stop our own mouths: we deserve nothing

and therefore why should we be impatient if we do not get what we desire. If we had deserved anything we might be troubled, as in the case of a man who has deserved well of the state or of his friends, yet does not receive a suitable reward, it troubles him greatly, whereas if he is conscious that he has deserved nothing, he is content with a rebuff.

3. *I can do nothing*. Christ says, 'Without me you can do nothing' (John 15. 5). Why should I make much of it, to be troubled and discontented if I have not got this and that, when the truth is that I can do nothing? If you were to come to one who is angry because he has not got such food as he desires, and is discontented with it, you would answer him, 'I marvel what you do or what use you are!' Should one who will sit still and be of no use, yet for all that have all the supply that he could possibly desire? Do but consider of what use you are in the world, and if you consider what little need God has of you, and what little use you are, you will not be much discontented. If you have learned this lesson of self-denial, though God cuts you short of certain comforts, yet you will say, 'Since I do but little, why should I have much': this thought will bring down a man's spirit as much as anything.

4. *I am so vile that I cannot of myself receive any good*. I am not only an empty vessel, but a corrupt and unclean vessel: that would spoil anything that comes into it. So are all our hearts: every one of them is not only empty of good but is like a musty bottle that spoils even good liquor that is poured into it.

5. If God cleanses us in some measure, and puts into us some good liquor, some grace of his Spirit, yet *we can make use of nothing when we have it, if God but withdraws himself*. If God leaves us one moment after he has bestowed upon us the greatest gifts, and whatever abilities we can desire, if God should say, 'I will give you them, now go and trade', we cannot progress one foot further if God leaves us. Does God give us gifts and abilities? Then let us fear and tremble lest God should leave us to ourselves, for then how foully should we abuse those gifts and abilities. You

think other men and women have memory and gifts and abilities and you would fain have them – but suppose God should give you these, and then leave you, you would utterly spoil them.

6. *We are worse than nothing.* By sin we become a great deal worse than nothing. Sin makes us more vile than nothing, and contrary to all good. It is a great deal worse to have a contrariety to all that is good, than merely to have an emptiness of all that is good. We are not empty pitchers in respect of good, but we are like pitchers filled with poison, and is it much for such as we are to be cut short of outward comforts?

7. *If we perish we will be no loss.* If God should annihilate me, what loss would it be to anyone? God can raise up some-one else in my place to serve him in a different way.

Now put just these seven things together and then Christ has taught you self-denial. I may call these the several words in our lesson of self-denial. Christ teaches the soul this, so that, as in the presence of God on a real sight of itself, it can say: 'Lord, I am nothing, Lord, I deserve nothing, Lord, I can do nothing, I can receive nothing, and can make use of nothing, I am worse than nothing, and if I come to nothing and perish I will be no loss at all, and therefore is it such a great thing for me to be cut short here?' A man who is little in his own eyes will account every affliction as little, and every mercy as great. Consider Saul: There was a time, the Scripture says, when he was little in his own eyes, and then his afflictions were but little to him: when some would not have had him to be King but spoke contemptuously of him, he held his peace; but when Saul began to be big in his own eyes, then the affliction began to be great to him.

There was never any man or woman so contented as a self-denying man or woman. No-one ever denied himself as much as Jesus Christ did: he gave his cheeks to the smiters, he opened not his mouth, he was as a lamb when he was led to the slaughter, he made no noise in the street. He denied himself above all, and was willing to empty himself, and so he was the most contented that ever any was in the world; and the nearer we come to learning to deny ourselves as Christ did, the more contented shall we be, and by knowing much of our own vileness we shall learn to justify God. Whatever the Lord shall lay upon us, yet he is righteous for he has to deal with a most wretched creature. A discontented heart is troubled because he has no more comfort, but a self-denying man rather wonders that he has as much as he has. Oh, says the one, I have but a little; Aye, says the man who has learned this lesson of self-denial, but I rather wonder that God bestows upon me the liberty of breathing in the air, knowing how vile I am, and knowing how much sin the Lord sees in me. And that is the way of contentment, by learning self-denial.

8. But there is a further thing in self-denial which brings contentment. *Thereby the soul comes to rejoice and take satisfaction in all God's ways;* I beseech you to notice this. If a man is selfish and self-love prevails in his heart, he will be glad of those things that suit with his own ends, but a godly man who has denied himself will suit with and be glad of all things that shall suit with God's ends. A gracious heart says, God's ends are my ends and I have denied my own ends; so he comes to find contentment in all God's ends and ways, and his comforts are multiplied, whereas the comforts of other men are single. It is very rare that God's ways shall suit with a man's particular end, but always God's ways suit with his own ends. If you will only have contentment when God's ways suit with your own ends, you can have it only now and then, but a self-denying man denies his own ends, and only looks at the ends of God and therein he is contented. When a man is selfish he cannot but have a great deal of trouble and vexation, for if I regard myself, my ends are so narrow that a hundred things will come and jostle me, and I cannot have room in those narrow ends of my own. You know in the City what a great deal of stir there is in narrow streets: since Thames street is so narrow they jostle and wrangle and fight one with another because the place is so narrow, but in the broad streets they can go quietly. Similarly men who are selfish meet and so jostle with one another, one man is for self in one thing, and

another man is for self in another thing, and so they make a great deal of stir. But those whose hearts are enlarged and make public things their ends, and can deny themselves, have room to walk and never jostle with one another as others do. The lesson of self-denial is the first lesson that Jesus Christ teaches men who are seeking contentment.

II. *The vanity of the creature.* That is the second lesson in Christ's school, which he teaches those whom he would make scholars in this art: the vanity of the creature, that whatever there is in the creature has an emptiness in it. 'Vanity of vanities, all is vanity,' is the lesson that the wise man learned: the creature in itself can do us neither good nor hurt; it is all but as wind. There is nothing in the creature that is suitable for a gracious heart to feed upon for its good and happiness. My brethren, the reason why you have not got contentment in the things of the world is not because you have not got enough of them – that is not the reason – but the reason is, because they are not things proportionable to that immortal soul of yours that is capable of God himself. Many men think that when they are troubled and have not got contentment it is because they have but a little in the world, and that if they had more then they should be content. That is just as if a man were hungry, and to satisfy his craving stomach he should gape and hold open his mouth to take in the wind, and then should think that the reason why he is not satisfied is because he has not got enough of the wind; no, the reason is because the thing is not suitable to a craving stomach. Yet there is really the same madness in the world: the wind which a man takes in by gaping will as soon satisfy a craving stomach ready to starve, as all the comforts in the world can satisfy a soul who knows what true happiness means. You would be happy, and you seek after such and such comforts in the creature. Well, have you got them? do you find your hearts satisfied as having the happiness that is suitable to you? No, no, it is not here, but you think it is because you lack such and such things. O poor deluded man! it is not because you have not got enough of it, but because it is not the thing that is proportionable to the immortal soul that God has given you. Why do you lay out money for that which is not bread, and your labour for that which satisfieth not? (Isaiah 55. 2). You are mad people, you seek to satisfy your stomach with that which is not bread, you follow the wind; you will never have contentment. All creatures in the world say contentment is not in us, riches say, contentment is not in me, pleasure says, contentment is not in me; if you look for contentment in the creature you will fail. No, contentment is higher. When you come into the school of Christ, Christ teaches you that there is a vanity in all things in the world, and the soul which, by coming into the school of Christ, by understanding the glorious mysteries of the Gospel, comes to see the vanity of all things in the world, is the soul that comes to true contentment. I could give you an abundance of proverbs from Heathens which show the vanity of all things in the world, and they did not learn the vanity of the creature in the right school. But when a soul comes into the school of Jesus Christ, and there comes to see vanity in all things in the world, then such a soul comes to have contentment. If you seek contentment elsewhere, like the unclean spirit you seek for rest but find none.

III. A third lesson which Christ teaches a Christian when he comes into his school is this : *He teaches him to understand what is the one thing that is necessary, which he never understood before.* You know what he said to Martha : 'O Martha, thou cumberest thyself about many things, but there is one thing necessary.' Before, the soul sought after this and that, but now it says, I see that it is not necessary for me to be rich, but it is necessary for me to make my peace with God; it is not necessary that I should live a pleasurable life in this world, but it is absolutely necessary that I should have pardon of my sin; it is not necessary that I should have honour and preferment, but it is necessary that I should have God as my portion, and have my part in Jesus Christ, it is necessary that my soul should be saved in the day of Jesus Christ. The other things are pretty fine indeed, and I should be glad if God would give me them, a fine house, and income, and clothes, and advancement

[92]

for my wife and children: these are comfortable things, but they are not the necessary things; I may have these and yet perish for ever, but the other is absolutely necessary. No matter how poor I am, I may have what is absolutely necessary: thus Christ instructs the soul. Many of you have had some thoughts about this, that it is indeed necessary for you to provide for your souls, but when you come to Christ's school, Christ causes the fear of eternity to fall upon you, and causes such a real sight of the great things of eternity, and the absolute necessity of those things, that it possesses your heart with fear and takes you off from all other things in the world.

It is said of Pompey, that when he was carrying corn to Rome at a time of dearth, he was in a great deal of danger from storms at sea, but he said, 'We must go on, it is necessary that Rome should be relieved, but it is not necessary that we should live.' So, certainly, when the soul is once taken up with the things that are of absolute necessity, it will not be much troubled about other things. What are the things that disquiet us here but some by-matters in this world? And it is because our hearts are not taken up with the one absolutely necessary thing. Who are the men who are most discontented, but idle persons, persons who have nothing to occupy their minds? Every little thing disquiets and discontents them; but in the case of a man who has business of great weight and consequence, if all things go well with his great business which is in his head, he is not aware of meaner things in the family. On the other hand a man who lies at home and has nothing to do finds fault with everything. So it is with the heart: when the heart of a man has nothing to do, but to be busy about creature-comforts, every little thing troubles him; but when the heart is taken up with the weighty things of eternity, with the great things of eternal life, the things of here below that disquieted it before are things now of no consequence to him in comparison with the other—how things fall out here is not much regarded by him, if the one thing that is necessary is provided for.

IV. *The soul comes to understand in what relation it stands to the world.* By that I mean as follows, God comes to instruct the soul effectually through Christ by his Spirit, on what terms it lives here in the world, in what relation it stands. While I live in the world my condition is to be but a pilgrim, a stranger, a traveller, and a soldier. Now rightly to understand this, not only being taught it by rote, so that I can speak the words over, but when my soul is possessed with the consideration of this truth, that God has set me in this world, not as in my home but as a mere stranger and a pilgrim who is travelling to another home, and that I am here a soldier in my warfare, I say, a right understanding of this is a mighty help to contentment in whatever befalls one.

For instance, when a man is at home, if things are not according to his desire he will find fault and is not content; but if a man travels, perhaps he does not meet with conveniences as he desires – the servants in the house are not at his beck or are not as diligent as his own servants were, and his diet is not as at home, and his bed not as at home – yet this thought may moderate his spirit: I am a traveller and I must not be finding fault, I am in another man's house, and it would be bad manners to find fault in someone else's house, even though things are not as much to my liking as at home. If a man meets with bad weather, he must be content; it is travellers' fare, we say. Both fair weather and foul are the common travellers' fare and we must be content with it. Of course, if a man were at home and the rain poured into his house, he would regard it as an intolerable hardship; but when he is travelling, he is not so troubled about rain and storms. When you are at sea, though you have not as many things as you have at home, you are not troubled at it; you are contented. Why? Because you are at sea. You are not troubled when storms arise, and though many things are otherwise than you would have them at home you are still quieted with the fact that you are at sea. When sailors are at sea they do not care what clothes they have, though they are pitched and tarred, and but a clout about their necks, and any old clothes. They think of when they come home: then they shall have their fine silk stockings and suits, and laced bands, and such things, and shall be very fine. So they are contented while away, with the thought that it shall be different when they come home, and though they have nothing but salt meat, and a little hard fare, yet when they come to their houses then they shall have anything.

Thus it should be with us in this world, for the truth is, we are all in this world but as seafaring men, tossed up and down on the waves of the sea of this world, and our haven is Heaven; here we are travelling, and our home is a distant home in another world. Indeed some men have better comforts than others in travelling, and it is truly a great mercy of God to us in England that we can travel with such delight and comfort, much more so than they can in other countries, and through God's mercy we have as great comforts in our travelling to Heaven in England as in any place under Heaven. Though we meet with travellers' fare sometimes, yet it should not be grievous to us. The Scripture tells us plainly that we must behave ourselves here as pilgrims and strangers: 'Dearly beloved, I beseech you as strangers and pilgrims, abstain from fleshly lusts, which war against the soul' (1 Peter 2. 11). Consider what your condition is, you are pilgrims and strangers; so do not think to satisfy yourselves here. When a man comes into an inn and sees there a fair cupboard of plate, he is not troubled that it is not his own. – Why? Because he is going away. So let us not be troubled when we see that other men have great wealth, but we have not. – Why? We are going away to another country; you are, as it were, only lodging here, for a night. If you were to live a hundred years, in comparison to eternity it is not as much as a night, it is as though you were travelling, and had come to an inn. And what madness is it for a man to be discontented because he has not got what he sees there, seeing he may be going away again within less than quarter of an hour? You find the same in David: this was the argument that took David's heart away from the things of this world, and set him on other things: 'I am a stranger in the earth, hide not thy commandments from me'

(Psalm 119. 19). I am a stranger in the earth – what then? – then, Lord, let me have the knowledge of your commandments and it is sufficient. As for the things of the earth I do not set store by them, whether I have much or little, but hide not thy commandments from me, Lord, let me know the rule that I should guide my life by.

Then again, we are not only travellers but soldiers: this is the condition in which we are here in this world, and therefore we ought to behave ourselves accordingly. The Apostle makes use of this argument in writing to Timothy: 'Thou therefore endure hardness as a good soldier of Jesus Christ' (2 Timothy 2. 3). The very thought of the condition of a soldier is enough to still his disquiet of heart. When he is away, he does not enjoy such comforts in his quarters as he has in his own home: perhaps a man who had his bed and curtains drawn about him, and all comforts in his chamber, has now sometimes to lie on straw and he thinks to himself, I am a soldier and it is suitable to my condition. He must have his bed warmed at home, but he must lie out in the fields when he is a soldier, and the very thought of the condition in which he stands, calms him in all things. Yes, and he goes rejoicing, to think that this is only suitable to the condition in which God has put him. So it should be with us in respect of this world. What an unseemly thing it would be to see a soldier go whining up and down with his finger in his eye, complaining, that he does not have hot meat every meal, and his bed warmed as he did at home!

Now Christians know that they are in their warfare, they are here in this world fighting and combating with the enemies of their souls and their eternal welfare, and they must be willing to endure hardness here. A right understanding of this fact that God has put them into such a condition is what will make them content, especially when they consider that they are certain of the victory and that ere long they shall triumph with Jesus Christ; then all their sorrows shall be done away, and their tears wiped from their eyes. A soldier is content to endure hardness though he does not know that he shall have the victory, but a Christian knows himself to be a soldier, and knows that he shall conquer and triumph with Jesus Christ to all eternity. And that is the fourth lesson that Christ teaches the soul when he brings it to his school to learn the art of contentment: he makes him understand thoroughly the relation in which he has placed him to this world.

V. *Christ teaches us wherein consists any good that is to be enjoyed in any creature in the world.* We have taught before that there is a vanity in the creature, that is, considered in itself, yet though there is a vanity in the creature in itself, in respect of satisfying the soul for its portion, yet there is some goodness in the creature, some desirableness. Now wherein does this consist? It consists not in the nature of the creature itself, for that is nothing but vanity, but it consists in its reference to the first being of all things: this is a lesson that Christ teaches. If there is any good in wealth or in any comfort in this world, it is not so much that it pleases my sense or that it suits my body, but that it has reference to God, the first being, that by these creatures somewhat of God's goodness might be conveyed to me, and I may have a sanctified use of the creature to draw me nearer to God, that I may enjoy more of God, and be made more serviceable for his glory in the place where he has set me: this is the good of the creature. Oh, that we were only instructed in this lesson, and understood, and thoroughly believed this! No creature in all the world has any goodness in it any further than it has reference to the first infinite supreme good of all, that so far as I can enjoy God in it, so far it is good to me, and so far as I do not enjoy God in it, so far there is no goodness in any creature. How easy it would be, if we really believed that, to be contented!

Suppose a man had great wealth only a few years ago, and now it is all gone — I would only ask this man, When you had your wealth, in what did you reckon the good of that wealth to consist? A carnal heart would say, Anybody might know that: it brought me in so much a year, and I could have the best fare, and be a man of repute in the place where I live, and men regarded what I said; I might be clothed as I would, and lay up portions for my children: the good of my wealth consisted in this. Now such a man never came into the school of Christ to know in what the good of an estate consisted, so no marvel if he is disquieted when he has lost his estate. But when a Christian, who has been in the school of Christ, and has been instructed in the art of contentment, has some wealth, he thinks, In that I have wealth above my brethren, I have an opportunity to serve God the better, and I enjoy a great deal of God's mercy conveyed to my soul through the creature, and hereby I am enabled to do a great deal of good: in this I reckon the good of my wealth. And now that God has taken this away from me, if he will be pleased to make up the enjoyment of himself some other way, will call me to honour him by suffering, and if I may do God as much service now by suffering, that is, by showing forth the grace of his Spirit in my sufferings as I did in prosperity, I have as much of God as I had before. So if I may be led to God in my low condition, as much as I was in my prosperous condition, I have as much comfort and contentment as I had before.

Objection. You will say, it is true that if I could honour God in my low estate as much as in my prosperous estate then it would be something, but how can that be?

Answer. You must know that the special honour which God has from his creatures in this world is the manifestation of the graces of his Spirit. It is true that God gets a great deal of honour when a man is in a public place, and so is able to do a great deal of good, to countenance godliness, and discountenance sin, but the main thing is in our showing forth the virtues of him who has called us out of darkness into his marvellous light. If I can say that, through God's mercy in my affliction, I find the graces of God's Spirit working as strongly in me as ever they did when I had my wealth, I am where I was; indeed, I am in quite as good a condition, for I have the same good now that I had in my prosperous estate. I reckoned the good of it only in my enjoyment of God, and honouring of God, and now God has blessed the lack of it to stir up the graces of his Spirit in my soul. This is the work that God calls me to now, and I must consider God to be most honoured when I do the work that he calls me to; he set me to work in my prosperous estate to honour him at that time in that condition, and now he sets me to work to honour him at this time in this condition. God is most honoured when I can turn from one condition to another, according as he calls me to it. Would you account yourselves to be honoured by your servants, if when you set them about a work that has some excellence, they will go on and on, and you cannot get them off from it? However good the work may be, yet if you call them off to another work, you expect them to manifest enough respect to you, as to be content to come off from that, though they are set about a lesser work, if it is more useful to your ends. In the same way you were in a prosperous estate, and there God was calling you to some service that you took pleasure in; but suppose God said: 'I will use you in a suffering condition, and I will have you to honour me in that way.'? This is how you honour God, that you can turn this way or that way, as God calls you to it. Thus having learned this, that the good of the creature consists in the enjoyment of God in it, and the honouring of God by it, you can be content, because you have the same good that you had before, and that is the fifth lesson.

VI. *Christ teaches the soul whom he brings into this school in the knowledge of their own hearts.* You must learn this or you will never learn contentment. You must learn to know your own hearts well, to be good students of your own hearts. You cannot all be scholars in the arts and sciences in the world, but you may all be students of your own hearts. Many of you cannot read in the Book, but God expects you every day to turn over a leaf in your own hearts. You will never get any skill in this mystery of contentment, except you study the book of your own hearts. Sailors have their books which they study, those who will be good navigators, and scholars have their books, those who study Logic have their books according to that, and those that study Rhetoric and Philosophy have their books according to that, and those that study Divinity have their books whereby they come to be helped in the study of Divinity, but a Christian, next to the Book of God, is to look into the book of his own heart, and to read over that, and this will help you to contentment in three ways:

1. By studying your heart *you will come soon to discover wherein your discontent lies*. When you are discontented you will find out the root of any discontent if you study your heart well. Many men and women are discontented, and the truth is they do not know why; they think this and the other thing is the cause. But a man or woman who knows their own heart will soon find out where the root of their discontent lies, that it lies in some corruption and disorder of the heart, that through God's mercy I have now found out. It is similar to the case of a little child who is very awkward in the house, and when a stranger comes in he does not know what the matter is. Perhaps he will give the child a rattle, or a nut, or something of the sort to quiet it, but when the nurse comes she knows the temper and disposition of the child, and therefore knows how to calm it. It is just the same here: when we are strangers to our own hearts we are powerfully discontented, and do not know how to quiet ourselves, because we do not know wherein the disquiet lies, but if we are very well versed in our own hearts, when anything happens to unsettle us, we soon find out the cause of it, and so quickly become quiet. When a man has a watch, and understands the use of every wheel and pin, if it goes amiss he will soon find out the cause of it; but when someone has no skill in a watch, if it goes amiss he does not know what is the matter, and therefore cannot mend it. So indeed our hearts are as a watch, and there are many wheels and windings and turnings there, and we should labour to know our hearts well, that when they are out of tune, we may know what is the matter.

2. This knowledge of our hearts will help us to contentment, because by it *we shall come to know what best suits our condition*. A man who does not know his own heart does not think what need he has of affliction, and for that reason is uneasy, but when God comes with afflictions to the man or

[100]

woman who have studied their own hearts, they can say, 'I would not have been without this affliction for anything in the world, God has so suited this affliction to my condition, and has come in such a way that if this affliction had not come I am afraid I should have fallen into sin.' When a poor countryman takes medicine, the medicine works, but he thinks it will kill him, because he does not know the bad humours that are in his body, and therefore he does not understand how suitable the medicine is for him. But if a doctor takes a purge, and it makes him extremely sick: 'I like this the better' he says, 'it is only working on the humour that I know is the cause of my disease', and because of that such a man, who has knowledge and understanding of his body, and the cause of his disorder, is not troubled or disturbed. So would we be if we did but know the disorders of our own hearts. Carnal men and women do not know their own spirits, and therefore they fling and vex themselves at every affliction that befalls them, they do not know what disorders are in their hearts which may be healed by their afflictions, if it pleases God to give them a sanctified use of them.

3. By knowing their own hearts *they know what they are able to manage*, and by this means they come to be content. Perhaps the Lord takes away many comforts from them that they had before, or denies them some things that they hoped to have got. Now by knowing their hearts they know that they were not able to manage such wealth, and they were not able to manage such prosperity. God saw it, and, a poor soul says, 'I am in some measure convinced by looking into my own heart that I was not able to manage such a condition.' A man desires greedily to hold on to more than he is able to manage, and so undoes himself. Countrymen observe that if they over-stock their land, it will quickly spoil them, and so a wise husbandman who knows how much his ground will bear is not troubled that he has not as much stock as others – why? Because he knows he has not got enough ground for as great a stock, and that quiets him. Many men and women who do not know their own hearts would fain have as prosperous a posi-

tion as others, but if they knew their own hearts they would know that they were not able to manage it.

Suppose one of your little children of three or four were crying for the coat of her sister who is twelve or perhaps even twenty, and said, 'Why may not I have a coat as long as my sister's?' If she had, it would soon trip up her heels, and scratch her face. But when the child comes to understanding, she is not discontented because her coat is not as long as her sister's, but says, 'My coat fits me,' and therein she is content. So if we come to understanding in the school of Christ we will not cry, Why have I not got such wealth as others have?, but, The Lord sees that I am not able to manage it and I see it myself by knowing my own heart. There are some children who, if they see a knife, will cry for it because they do not know their strength and that they are not able to manage it, but you know they are not able to manage it and therefore you will not give it them, and when they come to sufficient understanding to know that they are not able to manage it, they will not cry for it. Similarly we would not cry for some things if we knew that we were not able to manage them. When you vex and fret for what you have not got, I may say to you as Christ said, 'You know not of what spirit you are.' It was a saying of Œcolampadius to Parillus, when they were speaking about his extreme poverty, 'Not so poor, though I have been very poor, yet I would be poorer; I could be willing to be poorer than I am.' As if he were to say, The truth is, the Lord knew what was more suitable for me, and I knew that my own heart was such that a poor condition was more suitable to me than a rich. So certainly would we say, if we knew our own hearts, that such and such a condition is better for me than if it had been otherwise.

6

HOW CHRIST TEACHES CONTENTMENT–
concluded

────────

VII. The seventh lesson by which Christ teaches contentment is *the burden of a prosperous outward condition*. One who comes into Christ's school to be instructed in this art never attains to any great skill in it until he comes to understand the burden that is in a prosperous condition.

Objection. You will say, 'What burden is there in a prosperous condition?'

Answer. Yes, there is certainly a great burden, and it needs great strength to bear it. Just as men need strong brains to bear strong wine, so they need strong spirits to bear prosperous conditions, and not to do themselves hurt. Many men and women look at the shine and glitter of prosperity, but they little think of the burden. There is a fourfold burden in a prosperous condition.

1. There is a burden of *trouble*. A rose has its prickles, and the Scripture says that he that will be rich pierceth himself through with many sorrows (1 Timothy 6. 10). If a man's heart is set upon being rich, such a man will pierce himself through with many sorrows: he looks upon the delight and glory of riches which appears outwardly, but he does not consider what piercing sorrows he may meet with in them. The consideration of the trouble that is in a prosperous condition, I have many times thought of, and I cannot think of anything better to compare it with than to travelling in some open country, where round about is very fair and sandy

ground, and you see a town a great way off in a valley and you think, Oh how well situated that town is; but when you come and ride into the town, you ride through a dirty lane and through a lot of fearfully dirty holes. You could not see the dirty lane and holes when you were two or three miles off. In the same way, sometimes we look upon the prosperity of men and think, this man lives well and comfortably, but if we only knew what troubles he has in his family, in his possessions, in his dealings with men, we would not think his position so happy. A man may have a very fine new shoe, but nobody knows where it pinches him except the one who has it on; so you think certain men are happy, but they may have many troubles that you little think of.

2. There is a burden of *danger* in it. Men in a prosperous position are in a great deal of danger. You see sometimes in the evening that when you light up your candles, the moths and gnats will fly up and down in the candle and scorch their wings, and they fall down dead there. So there is a great deal of danger in a prosperous estate, for men who are set upon a pinnacle on high are in greater danger than other men are. Honey, we know, invites bees and wasps to it, and the sweet of prosperity invites the Devil and temptation. Men in a prosperous position are subject to many temptations that other men are not subject to. The Scripture calls the Devil Beelzebub, that is, the God of flies, and so Beelzebub comes where the honey of prosperity is. Yes, they are in very great danger of temptations who are in a prosperous condition. The dangers that men in a prosperous position have more than others should be considered by those who are lower. Think to yourself: though they are above me, yet they are in more danger than I am. Tall trees are a great deal more broken than low shrubs, and you know when a ship has all its sails up in a storm, even the top sail, it is in more danger than one which has all its sails drawn in. Similarly, men who have their top sail and all up so finely, are more likely to be drowned, drowned in perdition, than other men. You know what the Scripture says, how hard it is for rich men to go into the

Kingdom of Heaven; such a text should make poor people content with their state.

We have a striking example of this in the children of Kohath: you will find that they were in a more excellent position than the other Levites, but they were in more danger than the others, and more trouble. That the children of Kohath were in a higher position than the other Levites I will show you from the fourth chapter of Numbers. There you find what their position was: 'This shall be the service of the sons of Kohath in the tabernacle of the congregation, about the most holy things.' Mark this, the Levites were exercised about holy things, but the service of the sons of Kohath was about the most holy things of all. And you find in the 21st of Joshua that God honoured the sons of Kohath in a more special manner than he honoured the other Levites, which honour the children of Aaron (being of the families of the Kohathites, who were of the children of Levi) had, for theirs was the first lot (Joshua 21. 10) and they were preferred before the other families of Levi. Those who were employed in the most honourable employment had the most honourable lot, the first lot fell to them. Thus you see how God honoured the children of the Kohathites. But the other Levites might say, 'How has God preferred this family before us?' They are indeed honoured more than the others. But notice the burden that comes with their honour; I will show you it out of two Scriptures. The first is Numbers 7. 6–9, 'And Moses took the wagons, and the oxen, and gave them unto the Levites, two wagons and four oxen he gave unto the sons of Gershom, according to their service, and four wagons and eight oxen he gave unto the sons of Merari according to their service, under the hand of Ithamar the son of Aaron the priest'; but in the ninth verse he says, 'Unto the sons of Kohath he gave none, because the service of the sanctuary that belonged unto them, was, that they should bear upon their shoulders.' Mark, the other Levites had oxen and wagons given to them, to make their service easier, but, he says, to the sons of Kohath he gave none, but they should bear their service on their shoulders. And that is the reason why God was so displeased, because they wanted more ease in God's service than God would have them, for whereas they should have carried it upon their shoulders, they would carry it upon a cart. Here you see the first burden that they had, beyond what the other Levites had. And indeed, those who are in a more honourable place than others have a burden to carry on their shoulders that those who are under them do not think of, while others have ways of easing their burden. Many times those who are employed in the ministry, or the magistracy, who sit at the stern to order the great affairs of the commonwealth and state, though you think they have a fine life, they lie awake when you are asleep. If you knew the burden that lay upon their spirits, you would think that your labour and burden were very little in comparison of theirs.

There is another burden of danger more than the rest, and you will find it in Numbers 4. 17: 'And the Lord spake unto Moses and unto Aaron saying, Cut ye not off the tribe of the families of the Kohathites from among the Levites, but thus do unto them that they may live and not die: When they approach unto the most holy things, Aaron and his sons shall go in and appoint them every one to his service and to his burden; but they shall not go in to see when the holy things are covered, lest they die.' Mark this text: the Lord says to Moses and Aaron, 'Cut ye not off the tribe of the families of the Kohathites from among the Levites', cut them not off – Why? What had they done? Had they done anything amiss? No, they had not done anything to provoke God; but the meaning is this: take great care to instruct the family of the Kohathites in the duty that they were to do, for, said God, they are in a great deal of danger, serving in the most holy things. If they go in to see the holy things more than God would have them do, it is as much as their lives are worth, and therefore, if you neglect them, and do not inform them thoroughly in their duty, they would be undone, said God. They are to administer in the most holy things, and if they should but dare to presume to do anything otherwise than God would have them, about those services, it would cost them their lives; and therefore do not be careless of them, for if you neglect them you will be a means of cutting them off. Thus you see the danger that the family of the Kohathites were in; they were preferred before others, but they were in more danger. So you think of certain men in a parish who bear the sway and are employed in public service, and carry all before them, but you do not consider their danger. And similarly ministers stand in the forefront of all the spite and malice of ungodly men; certainly God employs them in an honourable service, and a service that the angels would delight in, but though the service is honourable, above other works, yet the burden of danger is likewise greater than the danger of men in an inferior position. Now when the soul gets wisdom from Christ to think of the danger that it is in, then it will be content with the low estate in which it is. A poor man who is in a low condition, thinks, 'I am low and others are raised, but I know now what their burden is', and so, if he is rightly instructed in the school of Christ, he comes to be contented.

3. In a prosperous condition there is the burden of *duty*. You look only at the sweetness and comfort, the honour and respect that they have who are in a prosperous position, but you must consider the duty that they owe to God. God requires more duty at their hands than at yours. You are ready to be discontented because you have not got such gifts and abilities as others have, but God requires more duty of those who have greater wealth than of you who have not such wealth. Oh, you would fain have the honour, but can you carry the burden of the duty?

4. The last is the burden of *account* in a prosperous condition. Those who enjoy great wealth and a prosperous condition have a great account to give to God. We are all stewards, and one is a steward to a meaner man, perhaps but to an ordinary knight, another is a steward to a nobleman, an earl— now the steward of the meaner man has not so much as the other under his hand, and shall he be discontented because of this? No, he thinks, I have less, and I will have to give the less account. So your account, in comparison of the minister's

and magistrate's, will be nothing: you are to give an account of your own souls and so are they, you are to give an account for your own family and so are they, but you will not have to give account for congregations, and for towns, and cities and countries. You think of princes and kings – Oh, what a glorious position they are in! But what do you think of a king who has to give account for the disorder and wickedness in a kingdom which he might possibly have prevented? What an abundance of glory might a prince bring to God if he bent his soul and all his thoughts to lift up the name of God in his kingdom! Now what God loses through the lack of this, that king, prince or governor must give an account for. There is a saying of Chrysostom on that place in Hebrews where it is said that men must give an account or their souls: he wonders that any man in a public place can be saved, because the account they have to give is so great. I remember I have read a saying of Philip, the King of Spain: though the story says of him that he had such a natural conscience that he professed he would not do anything against his conscience, no, not in secret, for gaining a world, yet when this man was to die, 'Oh', he said, 'that I had never been a king! Oh, that I had lived a solitary and private life all my days! Then I should have died a great deal more securely, I should with more confidence have gone before the throne of God to give my account. This is the fruit of my kingdom, because I had all the glory of it, it has made my account harder to give to God'. Thus he cried out when he was to die.

And therefore you who live in private positions, remember this: if you come to Christ's school and are taught this lesson, you will be quiet in your afflictions, or in your private position, because your account is not as great as others. There is a saying I remember meeting with in Latimer's sermons which he was wont to use: 'The half is more than the whole'; that is, when a man is in a mean condition, he is but half way towards the height of prosperity that others are in, yet, he says, this is safer though it is a meaner condition than others.

Those who are in a high and prosperous condition have

[108]

annexed to it the burden of trouble, of danger, of duty, and of account. And thus you see how Christ trains up his scholars in his school, and though they are otherwise weak, yet by his Spirit he gives them wisdom to understand these things aright.

VIII. *Christ teaches them what a great and dreadful evil it is to be given up to one's heart's desires.* It is, indeed, a dreadful evil, one of the most hideous and fearful evils that can befall any man on the face of the earth, for God to give him up to his heart's desires. A kindred truth is that spiritual judgments are more fearful than any outward judgments. Now once the soul understands these things, a man will be content when God crosses him in his desires. You are crossed in your desires, and so you are discontented and vexed and fretted about it; is that your only misery, that you are crossed in your desires? No, no, you are infinitely mistaken; the greatest misery of all is for God to give you up to your heart's lusts and desires, to give you up to your own counsels. So you have it in Psalm 81. 11, 12: 'But my people would not hearken to my voice, and Israel would none of me,' – what then? – 'So I gave them up unto their own heart lust, and they walked in their own counsels.' 'Oh let me not have such a misery as that', said Bernard, 'for to give me what I would have, to give me my heart's desires is one of the most hideous judgments in the world.'

In Scripture we have no certain, evident sign of a reprobate, we cannot say, unless we knew a man had committed the sin against the Holy Ghost, that he is a reprobate, for we do not know what God may work upon him, but the nearest of all and the blackest sign of a reprobate is this: for God to give a man up to his heart's desires. All the pain of diseases, all the calamities that can be thought of in the world are no judgments in comparison of this. Now when the soul comes to understand this, it cries out, why am I so troubled that I have not got my desires? There is nothing that God conveys his wrath more through than a prosperous condition. I remember reading of a Jewish tradition about Uzziah: when God struck him with leprosy, they say that the beams of the sun darted upon the forehead of Uzziah, and he was struck with leprosy in this way. The Scripture says, indeed, that the priests looked upon him, but they say that there was a special light and beam of the sun on his forehead that revealed the leprosy to the priests, and they say that was the way of conveying of it. Whether that was true or not, I am sure that this is true, that the strong beams of the sun of prosperity upon many men make them to be leprous. Would any poor man in the country have been discontented that he was not in Uzziah's position? He was a great King, aye, but there was the leprosy in his forehead. The poor man might say, Though I live meanly in the country yet I thank God my body is whole and sound. Would not any man rather have homespun and skins of beasts to clothe himself with, than to have satin and velvet that had plague in it? The Lord conveys the plague of his curse through prosperity, as much as through any thing in the world, and therefore when the soul comes to understand this, this makes it quiet and content.

And then, spiritual judgments are the greatest judgments of all. The Lord lays such and such an affliction upon my outward wealth, but what if he had taken away my life? A man's health is a greater mercy than his wealth, and you poor people should consider that. Is the health of a man's body better than his wealth? What then is the health of a man's soul? That is a great deal better. The Lord has inflicted external judgments, but he has not inflicted spiritual judgments on you, he has not given you up to hardness of heart, and taken away the spirit of prayer from you in your afflicted condition. Oh, then, be of good comfort though you have outward afflictions upon you; still your soul, your more excellent part is not afflicted. Now when the soul comes to understand this, that here lies the sore wrath of God, to be given up to one's desires, and to have spiritual judgments: this quiets him, and contents him, though outward afflictions are on him. Perhaps one of a man's children has the fit of an ague or toothache, but his next door neighbour has the plague, or all his children have died of it.

Now shall he be so discontented that his children have tooth-ache when his neighbour's children are dead? Think thus: Lord, you have laid an afflicted condition upon me, but, Lord, you have not given me the plague of a hard heart.

Now if you take these eight things before mentioned, and lay them together, you may well apply that Scripture in the 29th of Isaiah, the last verse, where it says, 'They also that erred in spirit shall come to understanding; and they that murmured shall learn doctrine.' Have there been any of you, as I fear many may be found, who have erred in spirit, even in regard of this truth that we are now preaching of, and many who have murmured? Oh, that this day you might come to understand, that Christ would bring you into his school, and teach you understanding. 'And they that murmured shall learn doctrine' – what doctrine shall they learn? These doctrines that I have opened to you. And if you will but thoroughly study these lessons that I have set before your eyes, it will be a special help and means to cure your murmurings and repinings at the hand of God, and so you will come to learn Christian contentment. The Lord teach you thoroughly by his Spirit these lessons of contentment!

I will only add one more lesson in the learning of contentment and then I shall come to the fourth head, the excellence of contentment.

IX. The ninth and last lesson which Christ teaches those whom he instructs in this art of contentment is *the right knowledge of God's providence*, and therein are four things.

1. *The universality of providence*, wherein the soul must be thoroughly instructed in to come to this art of contentment. To understand the universality of providence, that is, how the providence of God goes through the whole world and extends itself to everything. Not only that God by his providence rules the world, and governs all things in general, but that it reaches to every detail; not only to order the great affairs of kingdoms, but it reaches to every man's family; it reaches to every person in the family; it reaches to every condition; yea, to every happening, to everything that falls out concerning you in every

particular: not one hair falls from your head, not a sparrow to the ground, without the providence of God. Nothing befalls you, good or evil, but there is a providence of the infinite eternal first Being in that thing; and therein is God's infiniteness, that it reaches to the least things, to the least worm that is under your feet. Then much more does it reach to you who are a rational creature; the providence of God is more special towards rational creatures than any others. Now to understand in a spiritual way the universality of providence in every particular happening from morning to night every day, that there is nothing that befalls you but there is a hand of God in it – this is from God, and is a great help to contentment. Every man will grant the truth of the thing, that it is so, but as the Apostle says, in Hebrews 11. 3: 'By faith we understand that the worlds were made'; by faith we understand it. Why by faith? we can understand by reason that no finite thing can be from itself, and therefore that the world could not be of itself, but we understand it by faith in another way than by reason. So whatever we understand of God in providence, yet when Christ takes us into his school we come to understand it by faith in a better manner than we do by reason.

2. *The efficacy that is in providence.* That is, that the providence of God goes on in all things, with strength and power, and will not to be altered by our power. Suppose we are discontented and vexed and troubled, and we fret and rage, yet we need not think we will alter the course of providence by our discontent. Some of Job's friends, when they saw that he was impatient, said to him: 'Shall the earth be forsaken for thee? and shall the rock be removed out of his place?' (Job. 18. 4). So I may say to every discontented, impatient heart: what, shall the providence of God change its course for you? Do you think it such a weak thing, that because it does not please you it must alter its course? Whether or not you are content the providence of God will go on, it has an efficacy of power, of virtue, to carry all things before it. Can you make one hair black or white with all the stir that you are making? When you are in a ship at sea which has all its sails spread with a

full gale of wind, and is swiftly sailing, can you make it stand still by running up and down in the ship? No more can you make the providence of God alter and change its course with your vexing and fretting; it will go on with power, do what you can. Do but understand the power and efficacy of providence and it will be a mighty means helping you to learn this lesson of contentment.

3. *The infinite variety of the works of providence, and yet the order of things, one working towards another.* There is an infinite variety of the works of God in an ordinary providence, and yet they all work in an orderly way. We put these two things together, for God in his providence causes a thousand thousand things to depend one upon another. There are an infinite number of wheels, as I may say, in the works of providence; put together all the works that ever God did from all eternity or ever will do, and they all make up but one work, and they have been as several wheels that have had their orderly motion to attain the end that God from all eternity has appointed.

We, indeed, look at things by pieces, we look at one detail and do not consider the relation that one thing has to another, but God looks at all things at once, and sees the relation that one thing has to another. When a child looks at a clock, it looks first at one wheel, and then at another wheel: he does not look at them all together or the dependence that one has upon another; but the workman has his eyes on them all together and sees the dependence of all, one upon another: so it is in God's providence. Now notice how this works to contentment: when a certain passage of providence befalls me, that is one wheel, and it may be that if this wheel were stopped, a thousand other things might come to be stopped by this. In a clock, stop but one wheel and you stop every wheel, because they are dependent upon one another. So when God has ordered a thing for the present to be thus and thus, how do you know how many things depend upon this thing? God may have some work to do twenty years hence that depends on this passage of providence that falls out this day or this week.

And here, by the way, we may see what a great deal of evil there is in discontent, for you would have God's providence altered in such and such a detail: now if it were only in that detail, and that had relation to nothing else it would not be so much, but by your desire to have your will in such a detail, you may cross God in a thousand things that he has to bring about, because it is possible that a thousand things may depend upon that one thing that you would fain have otherwise than it is. It is just as if a child should cry out and say, 'Let that one wheel stop'; though he says only one wheel, yet if that were to stop, it is as much as if he should say they must all stop. So in providence: let but this one passage of providence stop—it is as much as if a thousand stopped. Let me therefore be quiet and content, for though I am crossed in some one particular thing God attains his end; at least, his end may be furthered in a thousand things by this one thing that I am crossed in. Therefore let a man consider, this is an act of providence, and how do I know what God is about to do, and how many things depend upon this providence? Now we are willing to be crossed in one thing, so that our friend may attain to what he desires in a thousand things. If you have a love and friendship to God, be willing to be crossed in a few things, that the Lord may have his work go on in general, in a thousand other things. Now that is the third thing to be understood in God's providence, which Christ teaches those whom he instructs in the art of contentment.

4. Christ teaches them the knowledge of providence, that is, *The knowledge of God's usual way in his dealings with his people more particularly*. The other is the knowledge of God in his providence in general. But the right understanding of the way of God in his providence towards his people and saints is a notable lesson to help us in the art of contentment. If we once get to know a man's way and course we may better suit, and be content to live with him, than before we got to know his way and course. When we come to live in a society with men and women, the men and women may be good, but till we come to know their way and course and disposition,

many things may cross us, and we think they are very hard, but when we come to be acquainted with their way and spirits, then we can suit and cotton with them very well; the reason of our trouble is because we do not understand their way. So it is with you : those who are but as strangers to God, and do not understand the way of God are troubled with the providences of God, and they think them very strange and cannot tell what to make of them, because they do not understand the ordinary course and way of God towards his people. Sometimes if a stranger comes into a family and sees certain things done, he wonders what is the matter, but those who are acquainted with it are not at all troubled by it. When servants first come together and do not know one another, they may be froward and discontented, but when they get to be acquainted with one another's ways, then they are more contented; just so it is when we first come to understand God's ways.

But you will say, What do you understand by God's ways?

By that I mean three things, and when we get to know them we shall not wonder so much at the providence of God, but be quiet and contented with them :

i. *God's ordinary course is that his people in this world should be in an afflicted condition.* God has revealed in his Word, and we may there find he has set it down as his ordinary way even from the beginning of the world to this day, but more especially in the times of the Gospel, that his people here should be in an afflicted condition. Now men who do not understand this stand and wonder to hear that the people of God are afflicted, and their enemies prosper in their way. When those who seek God in his way and seek for reformation are afflicted, wounded and spoiled, and their enemies prevail, they wonder at it; but one who is in the school of Christ is taught by Jesus Christ that God by his eternal counsels has set this as his course and way, to bring up his people in this world in an afflicted condition. Therefore the Apostle says, 'Account it not strange concerning the fiery trial' (1 Peter 4. 12). We are not therefore to be discontented with it, seeing God has set such a course and way, and we know it is the will of God that it should be so.

ii. *Usually when God intends the greatest mercy to any of his people he brings them into the lowest condition.* God seems to go quite across and work in a contrary way: when he intends the greatest mercies to his people he first usually brings them into very low conditions. If it is a bodily mercy, an outward mercy that he intends to bestow, he brings them physically low, and outwardly low; if it is a mercy in their possessions that he intends to bestow, he brings them low in that and then raises them; and in their reputations, he brings them low there, and then raises them; and in their spirits God ordinarily brings their spirits low and then raises their spirits. Usually the people of God, before the greatest comforts, have the greatest afflictions and sorrows. Now those who understand God's ways think that when God brings his people into sad conditions, he is leaving and forsaking them, and that God does not intend any great good to them. But a child of God, who is instructed in this way of God, is not troubled; 'My condition is very low,' he says, 'but this is God's way when he intends the greatest mercy, to bring men under the greatest afflictions.' When he intended to raise Joseph to be second in the kingdom, God cast him into a dungeon a little before. So when God intended to raise David and set him upon the throne, he made him to be hunted as a partridge in the mountains (1 Samuel 26. 20). God dealt this way with his Son: Christ himself went into glory by suffering (Hebrews 2. 10); and if God so deals with his own Son, much more with his people. A little before daybreak you will observe it is darker than it was any time before, so God will make our conditions a little darker before the mercy comes. When God bestowed the last great mercy at Naseby[1] we were in a very low condition; God knew what he had to do beforehand, he knew that his time was coming for great mercies: it is the way of God to do so. Be but instructed aright in this course and way that

[1] In 1645, the parliamentary army won a decisive victory against the Royalists at Naseby, Northamptonshire. The sermons which comprise this book were preached by Burroughs in this same year.

God is accustomed to walk in and that will greatly help us to contentment.

iii. *It is the way of God to work by contraries, to turn the greatest evil into the greatest good.* To grant great good after great evil is one thing, and to turn great evil into the greatest good is another, and yet that is God's way: the greatest good that God intends for his people, he many times works out of the greatest evil, the greatest light is brought out of the greatest darkness. I remember, Luther has a striking expression for this: he says, 'It is the way of God: he humbles that he might exalt, he kills that he might make alive, he confounds that he might glorify.' This is the way of God, he says, but every one does not understand it. This is the art of arts, and the science of sciences, the knowledge of knowledges, to understand this, that God when he will bring life, brings it out of death, he brings joy out of sorrow, and he brings prosperity out of adversity, yea and many times brings grace out of sin, that is, makes use of sin to work furtherance of grace. It is the way of God to bring all good out of evil, not only to overcome the evil, but to make the evil work toward the good. Now when the soul comes to understand this, it will take away our murmuring and bring contentment into our spirits. But I fear there are but few who understand it aright; perhaps they read of such things, and hear such things in a sermon, but they are not instructed in this by Jesus Christ, that this is the way of God, to bring the greatest good out of the greatest evil.

7

THE EXCELLENCE OF CONTENTMENT

Having concluded our study of the lessons we are to learn, we come to the next sub-division, which is, *the excellence of this grace of contentment*. There is, indeed, a great deal of excellence in contentment; that is, as it were, another lesson for us to learn.

The apostle says 'I have learned', as if he should say: Blessed be God for this! Oh! it is a mercy of God to me that I have learned this lesson, I find so much good in this contentment, that I would not for a world be without it. 'I have learned it', he says.

Now even the heathen philosophers had a sight of the great excellence that is in contentment. I remember reading of Antisthenes, who desired of his gods (speaking after the heathenish way) nothing in this world to make his life happy but contentment, and if he might have anything that he would desire to make his life happy, he would ask of them that he might have the spirit of Socrates, to be able to bear any wrong, any injuries that he met with, and to continue in a quiet temper of spirit whatsoever befell him; for that was the temper of Socrates: whatever befell him he continued the same man, whatever cross befell him, however great, nobody could perceive any alteration of his spirit. This a heathen attained to by the strength of nature, and a common work of the Spirit. Now Antisthenes saw such an excellence in this spirit that, as Solomon when God said to him: 'What shall I give thee?' asked of him wisdom, so he said: 'If the gods should put it to me to know what I would have, I would desire this thing, that I might have the spirit of Socrates.' He saw what a great excellence there was in this; and certainly a Christian may see an abundance of excellence in it. I shall labour to set it out to you in this chapter that you might be in love with this grace of contentment.

1. *By contentment we come to give God the worship that is due to him.* It is a special part of the divine worship that we owe to God, to be content in a Christian way, as has been shown to you. I say it is a special part of the divine worship that the creature owes to the infinite Creator, in that I tender the respect that is due from me to the Creator. The word that the Greeks have that signifies, 'to worship' is the same as to come and crouch before someone, as if a dog should come crouching to you, and be willing to lie down at your feet. So the creature in the apprehension of its own baseness, and the infinite excellence that is in God above it, when it comes to worship God, comes and crouches to this God, and lies down at the feet of God: then the creature worships God. When you see a dog come crouching to you, and by holding your hand over him, you can make him lie down at your feet, then consider, thus should you do before the Lord: you should come crouching to him, and lie down at his feet, even on your backs or bellies, to lie down in the dust before him so as to be willing that he should do with you what he will. Just as sometimes you may turn a dog this way or that way, up and down, with your hand, and there he lies before you, according to your showing him with your hand; so when the creature shall come and lie down thus before the Lord, then a creature worships God and tenders the worship that is due to him. Now in what disposition of heart do we thus crouch to God more than when we have this state of contentment in all the conditions that God disposes us to? This is crouching to God's disposal, to be like the poor woman of Canaan, who when Christ said, 'It is not fit to give children's meat to dogs', said 'The dogs have crumbs', I am a dog I confess, but let me have only a crumb. And so when the soul shall be in such a disposition as

to lie down and say, 'Lord, I am but as a dog, yet let me have a crumb', then it highly honours God. It may be that some of you have not your table spread as others have, but God gives you crumbs; now, says the poor woman, dogs have crumbs, and when you can find your hearts thus submitting to God, to be but as a dog, and can be contented and bless God for any crumb, I say this is a great worship of God.

You worship God more by this than when you come to hear a sermon, or spend half an hour, or an hour, in prayer, or when you come to receive a sacrament. These are the acts of God's worship, but they are only external acts of worship, to hear and pray and receive sacraments. But this is the soul's worship, to subject itself thus to God. You who often will worship God by hearing, and praying, and receiving sacraments, and yet afterwards will be froward and discontented — know that God does not regard such worship, he will have the soul's worship, in this subjecting of the soul unto God. Note this, I beseech you: in active obedience we worship God by doing what pleases God, but by passive obedience we do as well worship God by being pleased with what God does. Now when I perform a duty, I worship God, I do what pleases God; why should I not as well worship God when I am pleased with what God does? As it was said of Christ's obedience: Christ was active in his passive obedience, and passive in his active obedience; so the saints are passive in their active obedience, they are first passive in the reception of grace, and then active. And when they come to passive obedience, they are active, they put forth grace in active obedience. When they perform actions to God, then the soul says: 'Oh! that I could do what pleases God!' When they come to suffer any cross: 'Oh, that what God does might please me!' I labour to do what pleases God, and I labour that what God does shall please me: here is a Christian indeed, who shall endeavour both these. It is but one side of a Christian to endeavour to do what pleases God; you must as well endeavour to be pleased with what God does, and so you will come to be a complete Christian when you can do both, and that is the first thing in the excellence of this grace of contentment.

II. *In contentment there is much exercise of grace.* There is much strength of grace, yea, there is much beauty of grace in contentment; there is much exercise of grace, strength of grace, and beauty of grace: I put all these together.

1. *Much exercise of grace.* There is a compound of grace in contentment: there is faith, and there is humility, and love, and there is patience, and there is wisdom, and there is hope; almost all graces are compounded. It is an oil which has the ingredients of every kind of grace; and therefore, though you cannot see the particular grace, yet in this oil you have it all. God sees the graces of his Spirit exercised in a special manner, and this pleases God at the heart to see the graces of his Spirit exercised. In one action that you do you may exercise one grace especially, but in contentment you exercise a great many graces at once.

2. *There is a great deal of strength of grace in contentment.* It argues a great deal of strength in the body for it to be able to endure hard weather and whatever comes, and yet not to be much altered by it; so it argues strength of grace to be content. You who complain of weakness of memory, of weakness of gifts, you cannot do what others do in other things; but have you this gracious heart-contentment, that has been explained to you? I know that you have attained to strength of grace in this, when it is as spiritual as has been shown to you in the explication of this point. If a man is distempered in his body, and has many obstructions, has an ill stomach, and his spleen and liver obstructed, and yet for all this his brain is not disordered, it is an argument of a great strength of brain; though many evil fumes may arise from his corrupt stomach, yet still his brain is not disordered but he continues in the free exercise of his reason and understanding. Every one may understand that this man has a very strong brain, when such things do not upset him. If other people who have a weak brain do not digest but one meal's meat, the fumes that arise from their stomach disorder their brain and make them unfit

for everything, whereas these have strong heads, and strong brains, and though their stomachs are ill and they cannot digest meat, yet they still have the free use of their brain: this, I say, argues strength. So it is in a man's spirit: you find many who have weak spirits, and if they have any ill fumes, if accidents befall them, you will soon find them out of temper; but there are other men, who though things fume up, still keep in a steady way, and have the use of reason and of their graces, and possess their souls in patience.

I remember it is reported of the eagle that it is not like other fowls: when other fowls are hungry they make a noise; but the eagle is never heard to make a noise though it lacks food. Now it is from the magnitude of its spirit that it will not make such complaints as other fowls do when they lack food, because it is above hunger, and above thirst. Similarly it is an argument of a gracious magnitude of spirit, that whatsoever befalls it, yet it is not always whining and complaining as others do, but it goes on in its way and course, and blesses God, and keeps in a constant tenor whatever befalls it. Such things as cause others to be dejected and fretted and vexed, and take away all the comfort of their lives make no alteration at all in the spirits of these men and women. This, I say, is a sign of a great deal of strength of grace.

3. *It is also an argument of a great deal of beauty of grace.* There is a saying of Seneca, a heathen, 'When you go out into groves and woods, and see the tallness of the trees and their shadows, it strikes a kind of awful fear of a deity in you, and when you see the vast rivers and fountains and deep waters, that strikes a kind of fear of a God in you, but', he said, 'do you see a man who is quiet in tempests, and who lives happily in the midst of adversities, why do not you worship that man?' He thinks him a man worthy of such honour who will be quiet and live a happy life, though in the midst of adversities. The glory of God appears here more than in any of his works. There is no work which God has made – the sun, moon, stars and all the world – in which so much of the glory of God appears as in a man who lives quietly in the midst of adver-

sity. That was what convinced the king: when he saw that the three children could walk in the midst of the fiery furnace and not be touched, the king was mightily convinced by this, that surely their God was the great God indeed, and that they were highly beloved of their God who could walk in the midst of the furnace and not be touched, whereas the others who came only to the mouth of the furnace were devoured. So when a Christian can walk in the midst of fiery trials, without his garments being singed, and has comfort and joy in the midst of everything (when like Paul in the stocks he can sing, which wrought upon the jailor) it will convince men, when they see the power of grace in the midst of afflictions. When they can behave themselves in a gracious and holy manner in such afflictions as would make others roar: Oh, this is the glory of a Christian.

It is what is said to be the glory of Christ, (for it is thought by interpreters to be meant of Christ) in Micah 5. 5: 'And this man shall be the peace when the Assyrian shall come into our land, and when he shall tread in our palaces.' This man shall be the peace when the Assyrian shall come into our land – for one to be in peace when there are no enemies is no great thing, but the text says, when the Assyrian shall come into our land, then this man shall be the peace. That is, when all shall be in a hubbub and uproar, yet then this man shall be peace. That is the trial of grace, when you find Jesus Christ to be peace in your hearts when the Assyrian shall come into the land. You may think you find peace in Christ when you have no outward troubles, but is Christ your peace when the Assyrian comes into the land, when the enemy comes? Suppose you should hear the enemy come marching to the city and they had taken the works, and were plundering, what would be your peace? Jesus Christ would be peace to the soul when the enemy comes into the city, and into your houses. If any of you have been where the enemy has come, what has been the peace of your souls? What is said of Christ may be applied to this grace of contentment: when the Assyrian, the plunderers, the enemies, when any affliction, trouble, distress befalls such a heart, then this grace of contentment brings peace to the soul; it brings peace to the soul at the time when the Assyrian comes into the land. The grace of contentment is an excellent grace: there is much beauty, much strength in it, there is a great deal of worth in this grace, and therefore be in love with it.

III. *By contentment the soul is fitted to receive mercy, and to do service.* I will put these two together: contentment makes the soul fit to receive mercy, and to do service. No man or woman in the world is as fit to receive the grace of God, and to do the work of God, as those who have contented spirits.

Those who are contented are fitted to receive mercy from the Lord. If you want a vessel to take in any liquor, you must hold it still for if the vessel stirs and shakes up and down, you cannot pour in anything, but you will say, 'Hold still', that you may pour it in and not lose any. So if we would be vessels to receive God's mercy, and would have the Lord pour his mercy into us, we must have quiet, still hearts. We must not have hearts hurrying up and down in trouble, discontent and vexing, but still and quiet hearts, if we receive mercy from the Lord. If a child throws and kicks up and down for a thing, you do not give it him when he cries so, but first you will have the child quiet. Even though, perhaps, you intend him to have what he cries for, you will not give it him till he is quiet, and comes, and stands still before you, and is contented without it, and then you will give it him. And truly so does the Lord deal with us, for our dealings with him are just as your froward children's are with you. As soon as you want a thing from God, if you cannot have it you are disquieted at once and all in an uproar, as it were, in your spirits. God intends mercy to you, but he says, 'You shall not have it yet, I will see you quiet first, and then in the quietness of your hearts come to me, and see what I will do with you.' I appeal to you who are in any way acquainted with the ways of God, have you not found this to be the way of God towards you? When you were troubled for want, perhaps, of some spiritual comfort and your hearts were vexed at it, you got nothing from God all that while; but if you have got your heart into a quiet frame, and can say, 'Well, it is right that the Lord should do with his poor creatures what he will, I am under his feet, and am resolved to do what I can to honour him, and whatever he does with me, I will seek him as long as I live, I will be content with what God gives, and whether he gives or not I will be content.' 'Are you in this frame?' says God, 'now you shall have comfort, now I will give you the mercy.'

A prisoner must not think he will get rid of his chains by pulling and tearing; he may gall his flesh and rend it to the very bone, but certainly he will not be unfettered sooner. If he wants his fetters taken off he must quietly give up himself to some man to take them off. If a beggar knocks once or twice at the door and you do not come, and thereupon he is vexed and troubled and thinks it much that you let him stand a little while without anything, you think that this beggar is not fit to receive an alms. But if you hear two or three beggars at your door, and out of your window you hear them say, 'Let us be content to stay, perhaps they are busy, it is right that we should stay, it is well if we get anything in the end, we deserve nothing at all, and therefore we may well wait a while', you would then quickly send them an alms. So God deals with the heart: when it is in a disquiet mood then God does not give; but when the heart lies down quietly under God's hand, then is it in a fit frame to receive mercy. 'Your strength shall be to sit still,' says God, 'you shall not be delivered from Babylon but by your sitting still.'

IV. *As contentment makes fit to receive mercy, so fit to do service.* O the quiet fruits of righteousness, the peaceable fruits of righteousness! They indeed prosper and multiply most when they come to be peaceable fruits of righteousness. As the philosophers say of everything that moves, nothing moves but upon something that is immovable. A thing which moves upon the earth, could not move if the earth were not still.

Objection. The ships move upon the sea, and that is not still.

Answer. But the seas move upon that which is still and immovable. Nothing moves but it has something immovable that upholds it. The wheels in a coach move up and down, but the axle-tree does not move up and down; so it is with the heart of a man. As they say of the Heaven that it moves up and down upon a pole that is immovable, so it is in the heart of a man: if he will move to do service to God, he must have a steady heart within him. That must help him to move in the service of God, for those who have unsteady, disturbed spirits which have no steadfastness at all in them are not fit to do service for God, but such as have steadfastness in their spirits are men and women fit to do any service. That is the reason why, when the Lord has any great work for one of his servants to do, usually he first quiets their spirits, he brings their spirits into a quiet, sweet frame, to be contented with anything, and then he sets them about employment.

V. *Contentment delivers us from an abundance of temptations.* Oh, the temptations that men of discontented spirits are subject to! The Devil loves to fish in troubled waters. That is our proverb about men and women, their disposition is to fish in troubled waters, they say it is good fishing in troubled waters. This is the maxim of the Devil, he loves to fish in troubled waters; where he sees the spirits of men and women troubled and vexed, there the Devil comes. He says, 'There is good fishing for me', when he sees men and women go up and down discontented, and he can get them alone, then he comes with his temptations: 'Will you suffer such a thing?' he says, 'take this shift, this indirect way, do you not see how poor you are, others are well off, you do not know what to do for the winter, to provide fuel and get bread for you and your children', and so he tempts them to unlawful courses. This is the special disorder that the Devil fastens upon, when he gets men and women to give their souls to him: it is from discontent, that is the ground of all who have been witches, and so have given up themselves to the Devil: the rise of it has been their discontent. Therefore it is noticeable that those upon whom the Devil works, to make them witches, are usually old and melancholy people, and women especially, and those of the poorer sort who are discontented at home. Their neighbours trouble them and vex them, and their spirits are weak and they cannot bear it, so upon that the Devil fastens his temptations and draws them to anything. If they are poor, then he promises them money; if they have revengeful spirits, then he tells them that he will revenge them upon such and such persons: now this quiets and contents them. Oh! there is occasion of temptation for the Devil when he meets with a discontented spirit!

Luther said of God, 'God does not dwell in Babylon, but in Salem.' Babylon signifies confusion, and Salem signifies peace; now God does not dwell in spirits that are in a confusion, but he dwells in peaceable and quiet spirits. Oh, if you would free yourselves from temptations, labour for contentment. It is the peace of God that guards the heart from temptation. I remember reading of one Marius Curio who had bribes sent to him, to tempt him to be unfaithful to his country. When he was sitting at home at dinner with a dish of turnips, and they came and promised him rewards: said he, 'That man who can be contented with this fare that I have will not be tempted with your rewards. I thank God I am content with this fare, and as for rewards let them be offered to those that cannot be content to dine with a dish of turnips.'

So the truth is, as we see clearly, that the reason why many betray their trust, as in the service of Parliament and the Kingdom, is because they cannot be contented to be in a low condition. If a man is contented to be in a low condition, and to go meanly clothed if God sees fit, such a one is shot-free, you might say, from thousands of temptations of the Devil, that prevail against others to the damning of their souls. Oh, in such times as these, when men are in danger of the loss of their wealth, I say men who have not got this grace are in a most lamentable condition, they are in more danger for their souls than they are for their outward possessions. You think it is a sad thing to be in danger of your outward possessions that you may lose everything in a night; but if you have not this contented spirit within you, you are in more danger of the temptations of the Devil, to be plundered in that way of any good, and to be led into sin. Oh, when men think thus, that they must live as finely as they were wont to do, they make themselves a prey to the Devil, but for such as can say, 'Let God do with me what he pleases, I am content to submit to his hand in it', the Devil will scarcely meddle with such men. There was a notable saying of a philosopher who lived on mean fare: as he was eating herbs and roots, someone said to him, 'If you would but please Dionysius, you need not eat herbs and roots'; but he answered him thus, 'If you would but be content with such mean fare, you need not flatter Dionysius.' Temptations will no more prevail over a contented man, than a dart that is thrown against a brazen wall.

VI. The sixth excellence is *the abundant comforts in a man's life that contentment will bring*. Contentment will make a man's life exceedingly sweet and comfortable, nothing more so than the grace of contentment. I will show how it brings comfort in many ways.

1. What a man has *he has in a kind of independent way*, not depending upon any creature for his comfort.

2. *If God raises the position of a contented man who is low, he has the love of God in it*. It is abundantly more sweet then than if he had it and his heart was not contented; for God may grant a discontented man his desire, but he cannot say that it is from love. If a man has quieted his spirit first, and then God grants him his desire, he may have more comfort in it, and more assurance that he has the love of God in it.

3. This contentment is a comfort to a man's spirit in this, *that it keeps in his comforts, and keeps out whatever may damp his comforts, or put out the light of them*. I may compare this grace of contentment to a sailor's lantern: when a sailor is at sea, no matter how much provision he has in his ship, yet if he is thousands of leagues from land, or in a route where he will not meet with a ship for three or four months, he will be in a sad state if he has no lantern on his ship, nor anything by which to keep a candle alight in a storm. He would give a great deal to have a lantern, or something that might serve instead of one. When a storm comes in the night,

and he can have no light above board, but it is puffed out at once, his state is very sad. So, many men have the light of comfort when there is no storm, but let any affliction come, any storm upon them, and their light is puffed out at once, and what can they do now? When the heart is furnished with this grace of contentment, this grace is, as it were, the lantern, and it keeps comfort in the spirit of a man, light in the midst of a storm and tempest. When you have a lantern in the midst of a storm you can carry a light everywhere up and down the ship, to the top of the mast if you wish, and yet keep it alight; so when the comfort of a Christian is enlivened with the grace of contentment, it may be kept alight whatever storms or tempests come, still he can keep light in his soul. Oh this helps your comforts very much.

VII. *Contentment draws comfort from those things we do not really possess.* Perhaps many who have not got outward things have more comfort than those who do possess them. A man who distils herbs, though he has not got the herbs themselves, yet having the water that is distilled out of them, he may enjoy the benefit of the herbs. So though a man has not got real possession of such outward wealth, such an outward comfort, yet, by the grace of contentment he may get it to himself. By the art of navigation we can bring in the riches of the East and West Indies to ourselves; so by the art of contentment we may bring in the comfort of any condition to ourselves, that is, we may have that comfort by contentment, that we should have if we had the thing itself.

You will find a noteworthy story in Plutarch to illustrate this: In the life of Pyrrhus, one Sineus came to him, and would fain have had him desist from the wars, and not war with the Romans. He said to him, 'May it please your Majesty, it is reported that the Romans are very good men of war, and if it please the gods that we overcome them, what benefit shall we have of that victory?' Pyrrhus answered him, 'We shall then straightway conquer all the rest of Italy with ease.' 'Indeed that is likely which your Grace speaks,' said Sineus, 'but when we have won Italy, will our wars end then?'

'If the gods were pleased', said Pyrrhus, 'that the victory were achieved, the way would then be made open for us to attain great conquests, for who would not afterwards go into Africa, and so to Carthage?' 'But', said Sineus, 'when we have everything in our hands what shall we do in the end?' Then Pyrrhus laughing, told him again, 'We will then be quiet, and take our ease, and have feasts every day, and be as merry with one another as we possibly can.' Said Sineus, 'What prevents us now from being as quiet, and merry together, since we enjoy that immediately without further travel and trouble which we would seek for abroad, with such shedding of blood, and manifest danger? can you not sit down and be merry now?' So a man may think, if I had such a thing, then I would have another, and if I had that, then I should have more; and what if you had got all you desire? Then you would be content—why? You may be content now without them.

Certainly our contentment does not consist in getting the thing we desire, but in God's fashioning our spirits to our conditions. Some men have not got a foot of ground of their own, yet they live better than other men who are heirs to a great deal of land. I have known it in the country sometimes, that a man lives upon his own land, and yet lives very poorly; but you find another man who rents his land, and yet by his good husbandry, and by his care, lives better than he who has his own land. So a man by this art of contentment may live better without an estate than another man can live off an estate. Oh, it adds exceedingly to the comfort of a Christian.

That I may show it further I would add, there is more comfort even in the grace of contentment than there is in any possessions whatsoever; a man has more comfort in being content without a thing, than he can have in the thing that he in a discontented way desires. You think, if I had such a thing, then I should be content. I say, there is more good in contentment, than there is in the thing that you would fain have to cure your discontent, and that I shall show in several particulars:

1. I would fain have such a thing, and then I could be con-

tent; but if I had it, then it would be but the creature that helped my contentment, whereas now it is the grace of God in my soul that makes me content, and surely it is better to be content with the grace of God in my soul, than with enjoying an outward comfort?

2. If I had such a thing, granted my position might be better, but my soul would not be better; but by contentment my soul is better. That would not be bettered by wealth, or lands, or friends; but contentment makes myself better, and therefore contentment is a better portion than the thing that I would fain have as my portion.

3. If I become content by having my desire satisfied, that is only self-love, but when I am contented with the hand of God, and am willing to be at his disposal, that comes from my love to God. In having my desire satisfied, I am contented through self-love, but through the grace of contentment I come to be contented out of love to God, and is it not better to be contented out of love to God, than from a principle of self-love?

4. If I am contented because I have what I desire, perhaps I am contented in that one thing, but that one thing does not furnish me with contentment in another thing; perhaps I may grow more dainty and nice and froward in other things. If you give children what they want in some things, they grow so much the more coy and dainty and discontented if they cannot have other things that they want. But if I have once overcome my heart, and am contented through the grace of God in my heart, then this makes me content not only in one particular but in general, whatever befalls me. I am discontented, and would fain have a certain thing, and afterwards I have it: now does this prepare me to be contented in other things? No, but when I have got this grace of contentment, I am prepared to be contented in all conditions. Thus you see that contentment brings comfort to a man's life, fills it full of comfort in this world; the truth is, it is even a Heaven on earth. What is Heaven, but the rest and quiet of a man's spirit; that is the special thing that makes the life of Heaven, there is rest

and joy, and satisfaction in God. So it is in a contented spirit: there is rest and joy and satisfaction in God. In Heaven there is singing praises to God; a contented heart is always praising and blessing God. You have Heaven while you are on earth when you have a contented spirit; yea, in some regards it is better than Heaven.

How is that, you will say? There is a kind of honour that God has in it, and an excellence that he does not have in Heaven, and it is this: In Heaven there is no overcoming of temptations. They are not put to any trials by afflictions. In Heaven they have exercise of grace, but they have nothing but encouragement to it, and indeed the grace of those who are there is perfect, and in that they excel us. But there is nothing to cross their grace, they have no trials at all to tempt them to do contrary; whereas for a man or woman to be in the midst of afflictions, temptations and troubles, and yet to have grace exercised, and to be satisfied in God and Christ and in the Word and promises in the midst of all they suffer: this may seem to be an honour that God receives from us, that he does not have from the angels and saints in Heaven. Is it so much for one who is in Heaven, who has nothing but good from God, has nothing to try him, no temptations; is it so much for such a one to be praising and blessing God, as for the poor soul who is in the midst of trials and temptations and afflictions and troubles? For this soul to go on praying, and blessing, and serving God, I say, is an excellence that you do not find in Heaven, and God will not have this kind of glory from you in Heaven. Therefore be contented, and prize this contentment, and be willing to live in this world as long as God shall please. Do not think, Oh, that I were delivered from all these afflictions and troubles here in this world! If you were, then you would have more ease yourself, but this is a way of honouring God, and manifesting the excellence of grace here, when you are in this conflict of temptation, which God shall not have from you in Heaven.

So be satisfied and quiet, be contented with your contentment. I lack certain things that others have, but blessed be

[132]

God, I have a contented heart which others have not. Then, I say, be content with your contentment, for it is a rich portion that the Lord has granted you. If the Lord should give you thousands in this world, it would not be such a rich portion as this, that he has given you a contented spirit. Oh, go away and praise the name of God, and say, 'Why, Lord, it is true that I would be glad if I had these and these comforts which others have, but you have cut me short. Though I lack these, yet you have given me what is as good and better, you have given me a quiet, contented heart, to be willing to be at your disposal.'

VIII. *Contentment is a great blessing of God upon the soul.* There is God's blessing upon those who are content, upon them, and their possessions, and upon all that they have. We read in Deuteronomy of the blessing of Judah, the principal tribe: 'And he said, hear, Lord, the voice of Judah, and bring him unto his people, let his hands be sufficient for him, and be thou an help to him from his enemies.' Let his hands be sufficient for him, that is, bring a sufficiency of all good to him that he may have of his own: that is the blessing of Judah. So when God gives you a sufficiency of your own, as every contented man has, that is the blessing of God upon you, the blessing of the principal tribe, of Judah, is upon you. It is the Lord who gives us all things to enjoy; we may have the thing and yet not enjoy it unless God comes in with his blessing. Now whatever you have, you enjoy it; many men have possessions and do not enjoy them. It is the blessing of God which gives us all things to enjoy, and it is God who through his blessing has fashioned your heart and made it suitable to your circumstances.

IX. *Those who are content may expect reward from God, that God will give them the good of all the things which they are contented to be without.* This brings an abundance of good to a contented spirit. There is such and such a mercy which you think would be very pleasant to you if you had it; but can you bring your heart to submit to God in it? Then you shall have the blessing of the mercy one way or another;

if you do not have the thing itself, you shall have it made up one way or another; you will have a bill of exchange to receive something in lieu of it. There is no comfort that any soul is content to be without, but the Lord will give either the comfort or something instead of it. You shall have a reward to your soul for whatever good thing you are content to be without. You know what the Scripture says of active obedience: the Lord accepts of his servants their will for the deed. Though we do not do a good thing, yet if our hearts are upright, to will to do it, we shall have the blessing, though we do not do the thing. You who complain of weakness, you cannot do as others do, you cannot do as much service as others do—if your hearts are upright with God, and would fain do the same service that you see others do, and would account it a great blessing of God, the greatest blessing in the world if you were able to do as others do—now you may comfort yourselves with this, that dealing with God in the Covenant of grace, you shall have from God the reward of all you would do. As a wicked man shall have the punishment for all the sin he would commit, so you shall have the reward for all the good you would do. Now may not we draw an argument from active obedience to passive: there is as good reason why you should expect that God will reward you for all that you are willing to suffer, as well as for all that you are willing to do. If you are willing to be without such a comfort and mercy when God sees it fit, you shall be no loser; certainly God will reward you either with the comfort or with what shall be as good to you as the comfort. Therefore consider, How many things have I that others lack? and can I bring my heart into a quiet, contented frame to lack what others have? I have the blessing of all that they have, and I shall either possess such things as others have, or else God will make it up one way or another, either here or hereafter in eternity to me. Oh what riches are here! With contentment you have all kinds of riches.

X. Lastly, *by contentment the soul comes to an excellence near to God himself, yea, the nearest possible.* For this word,

[134]

that is translated 'content', signifies a self-sufficiency, as I told you in opening the words. A contented man is a self-sufficient man, and what is the great glory of God, but to be happy and self-sufficient in himself? Indeed, he is said to be all-sufficient, but that is only a further addition of the word 'all', rather than of any matter, for to be sufficient is all-sufficient. Now this is the glory of God, to be sufficient, to have sufficiency in himself. *El-shaddai* means to be God having sufficiency in himself. And you come near to this. As you partake of the Divine nature by grace in general, so you do in a more peculiar manner by this grace of Christian contentment, for what is the excellence and glory of God but this? Suppose there were no creatures in the world, and that all the creatures in the world were annihilated: God would remain the same blessed God that he is now, he would not be in a worse condition if all creatures were gone; neither would a contented heart, if God should take away all creatures from him. A contented heart has enough in the lack of all creatures, and would not be more miserable than he is now. Suppose that God should keep you here, and all the creatures that are in the world were taken away, yet you still, having God to be your portion, would be as happy as you are now. Therefore contentment has a great deal of excellence in it.

8

THE EVILS OF A MURMURING SPIRIT

Thus we have showed in many respects the excellence of this grace of contentment, labouring to present the beauty of it before your souls, that you may be in love with it. Now, my brethren, what remains but the practice of this? For this art of contentment is not a speculative thing, only for contemplation, but it is an art of divinity, and therefore practical. You are now to labour to work upon your hearts, that this grace may be in you, that you may honour God and honour your profession with this grace of contentment, for there are none who more honour God, and honour their profession than those who have this grace of contentment.

Now that we may come to grips with the practice, it is necessary that we should be humbled in our hearts because of our lack of contentment in the past. For there is no way to set about any duty with profit, till the heart is humbled for the lack of the performance of that duty previously. When you hear of a duty that you should perform, you might labour to perform it, but first you must be humbled for the lack of it. Therefore I shall endeavour to get your hearts to be humbled for lack of this grace. 'Oh, had I had this grace of contentment, what a happy life I might have lived! What abundance of honour I might have brought to the name of God! How might I have honoured my profession! What a great deal of comfort I might have enjoyed! But the Lord knows it has been far otherwise. Oh, how far have I been from this grace of contentment which has been expounded to me! I have had a murmuring, a vexing, and a fretting heart within me. Every little cross has put me out of temper and out of frame. Oh, the boisterousness of my spirit! What evil God sees in the vexing and fretting of my heart, and murmuring and repining of my spirit!' Oh that God would make you see it! Now to the end that you might be humbled for the lack of it, I shall endeavour in these headings to speak of it:

First I shall set before you *The evil of a murmuring spirit.* There is more evil in it than you are aware of.

In the second place, *I will show you some aggravations of this evil.* It is altogether evil, but more so in some cases than others.

Thirdly, *I shall labour to take away the excuses that any murmuring, discontented heart has for his disorder.*

There are these three things in this use of humbling of the soul for the want of this grace of contentment.

For the present, the first: *The great evil that is in a murmuring, discontented heart.*

I. *This murmuring and discontentedness of yours reveals much corruption in the soul.* As contentment argues much grace, and strong grace, and beautiful grace, so murmuring argues much corruption, and strong corruption, and very vile corruptions in your heart. If a man's body is of such a temper that every scratch of a pin makes his flesh to rankle and be a sore, you will surely say, this man's body is very corrupt, his blood and his flesh is corrupt, that every scratch of a pin shall make it rankle. So it is in your spirit, if every little trouble and affliction makes you discontented, and makes you murmur, and even causes your spirit within you to rankle. Or like a wound in a man's body, the evil of the wound is not so much in the largeness of it, and the abundance of blood that comes out of it, but in the inflammation that there is in it, or in a fretting and corrupting humour that is in the wound. When an unskilled man comes and sees a large wound in the flesh, he looks upon it as a dangerous wound, and when he sees a great deal of blood gush out, he thinks, these are the evils of it; but when a surgeon comes and sees a great gash, he says:

'This will be healed within a few days, but there is a smaller wound and an inflammation or a septic sore in it, and this will cost time', he says, 'to cure.' So he does not lay balsam and healing salves upon it, but his great care is to get out the septic inflammation, and the thing that must heal this wound is some potion to purge. But the patient says, 'What good will this do to my wound? You give me something to drink, and my wound is in my arm, or in my leg. What good will this do that I am putting in my stomach?' Yes, it purges out the infection, and takes away the inflammation, and till that is taken away the salves can do no good.

So it is, just for all the world, in the souls of men : it may be that there is some affliction upon them, which I compare to the wound; now they think that the greatness of the affliction is what makes their condition most miserable. Oh no, there is a fretting humour, an inflammation in the heart, a murmuring spirit that is within you, and that is the misery of your condition, and it must be purged out of you before you can be healed. Let God do with you what he will, till he purges out that fretting humour your wound will not be healed. A murmuring heart is a very sinful heart; so when you are troubled for this affliction you had need to turn your thoughts rather to be troubled for the murmuring of your heart, for that is the greatest trouble. There is an affliction upon you and that is grievous, but there is a murmuring heart within and that is more grievous. Oh, that we could but convince men and women that a murmuring spirit is a greater evil than any affliction, whatever the affliction! We shall show more fully afterward that a murmuring spirit is the evil of the evil, and the misery of the misery.

II. *The evil of murmuring is such that when God would speak of wicked men and describe them, and show the brand of a wicked and ungodly man or woman, he instances this sin in a more special manner.* I might name many Scriptures, but that Scripture in Jude is a most remarkable one. In the·14th verse onwards, it is said, 'That the Lord comes with ten thousands of his saints, to execute judgment upon all, and to convince all that are ungodly among them, of all their ungodly deeds, which they have ungodly committed, and of all their hard speeches, which ungodly sinners have spoken against him.' Mark here in this 15th verse mention is made four times of ungodly ones: all that are *ungodly* among them, all their *ungodly* deeds which they have *ungodly* committed, and of all their hard speeches which *ungodly* sinners have spoken against him. This is in general, but now he comes in particular to show who these are: 'These are', he says, 'murmurers',– that is the very first. Would you know who are ungodly men, whom God when he comes with ten thousand of angels shall come to punish for all their ungodly deeds that they do, and those that speak ungodly things against him? These ungodly ones are murmurers; murmurers in Scripture are put in the forefront of ungodly ones, and it is a most dreadful Scripture, that the Lord, when he speaks of ungodly ones, puts murmurers in the very forefront of all. You had need to look to your spirits; you may see that this murmuring, which is the vice contrary to this contentment, is not as small a matter as you think. You think you are not as ungodly as others, because you do not swear and drink as others do, but you may be ungodly in murmuring. It is true there is no sin but some seeds and remainders of it are in those who are godly; but when men are under the power of this sin of murmuring, it convicts them as ungodly, as well as if they were under the power of drunkenness, or whoredom, or any other sin. God will look upon you as ungodly for this sin as well as for any sin whatever. This one Scripture should make the heart shake at the thought of the sin of murmuring.

III. As well as being made a brand of ungodly men, you will find in Scripture *that God accounts it rebellion.* It is contrary to the worship that is in contentedness. That is worshipping God, crouching to God and falling down before him, even as a dog would crouch when you hold a stick over him; but a murmuring heart is a rebellious heart, as you will find, if you compare two Scriptures together: they are both in the book of Numbers. 'But on the morrow', says Numbers 16. 41, 'all the congregation of the children of Israel murmured against Moses and against Aaron, saying, Ye have killed the people of the Lord.' They all murmured; now compare this with chapter 17 and verse 10: 'And the Lord said unto Moses, Bring Aaron's rod again before the testimony, to be kept for a token against the rebels.' In the 16th chapter they murmured against Moses and Aaron, and in the 17th chapter we read, Bring the rod of Aaron again, before the testimony, for a token against the rebels. So you see that to be a murmurer, and to be a rebel, in Scripture phrase is all one; it is a rebellion against God. Just as it is the beginning of rebellion and sedition in a kingdom, when the people are discontented. When discontent comes, it grows to murmuring, and you can go into no house almost, but there is murmuring when men are discontented, so that within a little while it breaks forth into sedition or rebellion. Murmuring is but as the smoke of the fire: there is first a smoke and smouldering before the flame breaks forth; and so before open rebellion in a kingdom there is first a smoke of murmuring, and then it breaks forth into open rebellion. But because it has the seeds of rebellion, it is accounted before the Lord to be rebellion. Will you be a rebel against God? When you feel your heart discontented and murmuring against the dispensation of God towards you, you should check it thus: Oh, you wretched heart! What, will you be a rebel against God? Will you rise in rebellion against the infinite God? Yet you have done so. Charge your heart with this sin of rebellion. You who are guilty of this sin of murmuring, you are this day charged by the Lord, as being guilty of rebellion against him, and God expects that when you go home, you should humble your souls before him for this sin, that you should charge your souls for being guilty of rebellion against God. Many of you may say, I never thought that I was a rebel against God before, I thought that I had many infirmities, but now I see the Scripture speaks of sin in a different way than men do, the Scripture makes men, though only murmurers, to be rebels against God. Oh, this rebellious heart that I have against the Lord, which has manifested itself in this way of murmuring against the Lord! That is a third point in the evil of discontent.

IV. *It is a wickedness which is greatly contrary to grace, and especially contrary to the work of God, in bringing the soul home to himself.* I know no disorder more opposite and contrary to the work of God in the conversion of a sinner, than this is.

Question. What is the work of God when he brings a sinner home to himself?

Answer. 1. The usual way is for God to make the soul to see, and be sensible of the dreadful evil that is in sin, and the great breach that sin has made between God and it, for, certainly, Jesus Christ can never be known in his beauty and excellence till the soul knows that. I do not say what secret work of the Holy Ghost there may be in the soul, but before the soul can actually apply Jesus Christ to itself, it is impossible but that it must come to know the evil of sin, and the excellence of Jesus Christ. A seed of faith may be put into the soul, but the soul must first know Christ, and know sin, and be made sensible of it. Now how contrary is this sin of murmuring to any such work of God! Has God made me see the dreadful evil of sin, and made my soul sensible of the evil of sin as the greatest burden? How can I be then so much troubled for every little affliction? Certainly, if I saw what the evil of sin was, that sight would swallow up all other evils, and if I were burdened with the evil of sin, it would swallow up all other burdens. What! am I now murmuring against God's hand? says such a soul, whereas a while ago the Lord made me see myself to be a damned wretch, and apprehend it as a wonder that I was not in Hell?

2. Yea, it is strongly contrary to the sight of the infinite excellence and glory of Jesus Christ, and of the things of the Gospel. What! am I the soul to whom the Lord has revealed the infinite excellence of Jesus Christ, and yet shall I think such a little affliction to be so grievous to me, when I have had the sight of such glory in Christ as is worth more than ten thousand worlds? A true convert will say: 'Oh, the Lord at such a time gave me a sight of Christ that I would not be

without for ten thousand, thousand worlds.' But has God given you that, and will you be discontented for a trifle in comparison to that?

3. A third work when God brings the soul home to himself is by taking the heart off from the creature, disengaging the heart from all creature-comforts: that is the third work ordinarily that the soul may perceive of itself. It is true, God's work may be altogether in the seeds in him, but in the various actings of the soul, in turning to God, it may perceive these things in it. The disengagement of the heart from the creature is the calling of the soul from the world – 'whom the Lord hath called he hath justified' – what is the calling of the soul but this? The soul which before was seeking for contentment in the world, and cleaving to the creature, is now called out of the world by the Lord, who says: 'Oh Soul, your happiness is not here, your rest is not here, your happiness is elsewhere, and your heart must be loosened from all the things that are here below in the world.' This is the work of God in the soul, to disengage the heart from the creature, and how contrary is a murmuring heart to such a thing! Something which is glued to another cannot be taken off, but you must tear it; so it is a sign your heart is glued to the world, that when God would take you off, your heart tears. If God, by an affliction, should come to take anything in the world from you, and you can part from it with ease, without tearing, it is a sign then that your heart is not glued to the world.

4. A fourth work of God in converting a sinner is this, the casting of the soul upon Jesus Christ for all its good. I see Jesus Christ in the Gospel as the Fountain of all good, and God out of free grace tendering him to me for life and for salvation, and now my soul casts itself, rolls itself upon the infinite grace of God in Christ for all good. Now have you done so? Has God converted you, and drawn you to his Son to cast your soul upon him for all your good, and yet you are discontented for the want of some little matter in a creature comfort? Are you he who has cast your soul upon Jesus Christ for all good? As he says in another case, 'Is this thy faith?'

5. The soul is subdued to God. And then it comes to receive Jesus Christ as a King, to rule, to order, and dispose of him how he pleases, and so the heart is subdued unto God. Now how opposite is a murmuring, discontented heart to a heart subdued to Jesus Christ as a King, and receiving him as a Lord to rule and dispose of him as he pleases!

6. There is in the work of your turning to God the giving up of yourself to God in an everlasting covenant. As you take Christ, the head of the Covenant, to be yours, so you give up yourself to Christ. In the work of conversion there is the resignation of the soul wholly to God in an everlasting covenant to be his. Have you ever surrendered up yourself to God in an everlasting covenant? Then, certainly, this fretting, murmuring heart of yours is strongly opposite to it, certainly you forget this covenant of yours, and the resignation of yourself up to God. It would be of marvellous help to you to humble your souls when you are in a murmuring condition. If you could but obtain so much liberty of your own spirits as to look back to see what the work of God was in converting you, there is nothing would prevail more than to think of that. I am now in a murmuring, discontented way, but how did I feel my soul working when God turned my soul to himself! Oh, how opposite is this to that work, and how unbecoming! Oh, what shame and confusion would come upon the spirits of men and women, if they could but compare the work of corruption in their murmuring and discontent with the work of God that was upon their souls in conversion!

Now we should labour to keep the work of God upon our souls which was present at our conversion; for conversion must not be only at one instant at first. Men are deceived in this, if they think their conversion is finished merely at first; you must be in a way of conversion to God all the days of your life, and therefore Christ said to his disciples, 'Except ye be converted and become as little children?' Ye be converted. Why? Were they not converted before? Yes, they were converted, but they were still to continue the work of conversion all the days of their lives. What work of God there is at the first conversion is to abide afterwards. There must always abide some sight and sense of sin; it may be not in the way which you had, which was rather a preparation than anything else, but the sight and sense of sin is to continue still, that is, you are still to be sensible of the burden of sin as it is against the holiness, and goodness, and mercy of God to you. And the sight of the excellence of Jesus Christ is to continue, and your calling away from the creature, and your casting of your soul upon Christ, and your receiving Christ as a King – still receive him day by day – and the subduing of your heart, and the surrendering of yourself up to God in a way of covenant. Now if this were but daily continued, there would be no space nor time for murmuring to work upon your heart : that is the fourth point.

V. *Murmuring and discontent is exceedingly below a Christian.* Oh, it is too mean and base a disorder for a Christian to give place to it. Now it is below a Christian in many respects.

1. *Below the relation of a Christian.* How below the relation of a Christian? The relation in which you stand. Below what relation? you will say.

i. *The relation in which you stand to God.* Do you not call God your father? and do you not stand in relation to him as a child? What! do you murmur? In 2 Samuel 13. 4 there is a speech of Jonadab to Amnon : 'Why art thou, being the king's son, lean from day to day? wilt thou not tell me?'; and so he told him, but that was for a wicked cause. He perceived that his spirit was troubled, for otherwise he was of a fat and plump temper of body, but because of trouble of spirit he even pined away. Why? What is the matter? You stand in this relation to the King and yet let anything trouble your heart – that is his meaning; is there anything that should disquiet your heart when you stand in such a relation to the King, as the King's son?

So I may say to a Christian : Are you the King's son, the son, the daughter, of the King of Heaven, and yet so disquieted and troubled, and vexed at every little thing that happens? As if a King's son were to cry out that he is undone for losing a toy; what an unworthy thing would this be! So do you: you cry out as if you were undone and yet are a King's son, you who stand in such relation to God, as to a father, you dishonour your father in this; as if either he had not wisdom, or power, or mercy enough to provide for you.

ii. *The relation in which you stand to Jesus Christ*. You are the spouse of Christ. What! One married to Jesus Christ and yet troubled and discontented? Have you not enough in him? Does not Christ say to his spouse, as Elkanah said to Hannah: 'Am not I better to thee than ten sons?' (1 Samuel 1. 8). So does not Christ your husband say to you, 'Am not I better to you than thousands of riches and comforts, such comforts as you murmur for want of?' Has not God given you his Son and will he not with him give you all things? Has the love of God to you been such as to give you his Son in marriage? Why are you discontented and murmuring? Consider your relation to Jesus Christ, as a spouse and married to him: his person is yours, and so all the riches of Jesus Christ are yours, as the riches of a husband are his wife's. Though some husbands are so vile that their wives may be forced to sue for maintenance, certainly Jesus Christ will never deny maintenance to his spouse, it is a dishonour for a husband to have the wife go whining up and down. What! you are matched with Christ and are his spouse, and will you murmur now, and be discontented in your spirit? You will observe that with those who are newly married, when there is discontent between the wife and the husband, their friends will shake their heads and say, 'They are not meeting with what they expected; you see ever since they were married together how the man looks, and the woman looks, they are not so cheery as they used to be. Surely it is likely to prove an ill match.' But it is not so here, it shall not be so between you and Christ. Oh, Jesus Christ does not love to see his spouse with a scowling countenance; no man loves to see discontent in the face of his wife, and surely Christ does not love to see discontent in the face of his spouse.

iii. *You stand in relation to Christ, not only as a spouse, but as a member*. You are bone of his bone, and flesh of his flesh; and to have a member of Jesus Christ in a condition of discontent exceedingly unworthy.

iv. *He is your elder brother likewise*, and so you are a co-heir with him.

v. *The relation in which you stand to the Spirit of God*. You are the temple of the Holy Ghost, the Holy Ghost is your Comforter. It is he who is appointed to convey all comforts from the Father and the Son, to the souls of his people. And are you the temple of the Holy Ghost, and does he dwell in you, and yet for all that you murmur for every little thing?

vi. *The relation in which you stand to the angels*. You are made one body with them, for so Christ has joined principalities and powers with his Church: they are ministering spirits for the good of his people, to supply what they need, and you and they are joined together, and Christ is the head of you and angels.

vii. *The relation in which you stand to the saints*. You are of the same body with them, they and you make up but one mystical body with Jesus Christ, and if they are happy you must needs be happy.

Oh, how beneath a Christian is a murmuring spirit, especially when he considers the relations in which he stands!

2. A Christian should consider, *That murmuring and discontentedness is below the high dignity which God has put upon him*. Do but consider the high dignity which God has put upon you: the meanest Christian in the world is a lord of heaven and earth. He has made us kings unto himself, kings to God, not kings to men to rule over them; and yet I say, every Christian is lord of heaven and earth, yea of life and death. That is, as Christ is Lord of all, so he has made those who are his members lords of all. 'All are yours', says the Apostle, 'even life and death, every thing is yours.' It is a very strange expression, that death should be theirs, death is yours, that is, you are, as it were, lords over it, you have what shall make death your servant, your slave, even death itself, your greatest enemy is turned to be your slave. Faith makes a Christian as

lord over all, lifted up in excellence above all creatures that ever God made, except the angels, and in some respect above them.

I say the poorest Christian who lives is raised to a position above all the creatures in the world except angels, and above them in many respects too – and yet discontented! That you who were as a firebrand of hell, and might have been scorching and yelling and roaring there to all eternity, yet that God should raise you to have a higher excellence in you than there is in all the works of creation that ever he made except angels, and other Christians, who are in your position! Indeed, you are nearer the Divine nature than the angels, because your nature is joined in a hypostatical union to the Divine nature, and in that respect your nature is more honoured than the nature of the angels. And the death of Christ is yours. He died for you and not for the angels, and therefore you are likely to be raised above the angels in many respects. You who are in such a position as this, you who are set apart to the end that God might manifest to all eternity what the infinite power of a Deity is able to raise a creature to – for that is the position of a saint, a believer: his position is that he is set apart to the end that God might manifest to all eternity what his infinite power is able to do to make a creature happy.

Are you in such a position? Oh, how low and beneath this position is a murmuring and discontented heart for want of some outward comforts here in this world! How unseemly it is that you should be a slave to every cross, that every affliction shall be able to say to your soul, 'Bow down to us'! We accounted it a great slavery, when men said to our souls, 'Bow down', as the cruel prelates were wont to do, in imposing things upon men's consciences: in effect they said, 'Let your consciences, your souls, bow down to us, that we may tread upon them'. That is the greatest slavery in the world, that one man should say to another, 'Let your consciences, your souls, bow down, that we may tread upon them'; but will you allow every affliction to say, 'Bow down that we may tread upon you'? Truly it is so, when your heart is overcome with murmuring and discontent; know that those afflictions which have caused you to murmur have said to you, 'Bow down that we may tread upon you.' Nay, not afflictions, but the very Devil prevails against you in this. Oh! how this is beneath the happy position to which God has raised a Christian! What! will the son of a King let every base fellow come and bid him bow down, that he may tread upon his neck? That is what you do in every affliction: the affliction, the cross and trouble that befalls you, says, 'Bow down that we may come and tread upon you.'

3. *Murmuring is below the spirit of a Christian.* The spirit of every Christian should be like the spirit of his Father: every father loves to see his spirit in his child, loves to see his image, not the image of his body only, to say, here is a child for all the world like his father, but he has the spirit of his father too. A father who is a man of spirit loves to see his spirit in his child, rather than the features of his body. Oh, the Lord who is our Father loves to see his Spirit in us. Great men love to see great spirits in their children, and the great God loves to see a great spirit in his children. We are one spirit with God and with Christ, and one spirit with the Holy Ghost; therefore, we should have a spirit that might manifest the glory of the Father, Son and Holy Ghost in our spirits: that is the spirit of a Christian. The spirit of a Christian should be a lion-like spirit; as Jesus Christ is the Lion of the tribe of Judah (so he is called) so we should manifest something of the lion-like spirit of Jesus Christ. He manifested his lion-like spirit in passing through all afflictions and troubles whatsoever without any murmuring against God. When he came to drink that bitter cup, and even the dregs of it, he prayed indeed to God that if it were possible it might pass from him, but immediately: 'Not my will, but thy will be done.' As soon as ever he mentioned the passing of the cup from him, though it was the most dreadful cup that ever was drunk since the world began, yet at the mentioning of it: 'Not my will, but thy will be done.' Here Christ showed a lion-like spirit in going through all kinds of afflictions whatsoever, without any murmuring against God in

them. Now a murmuring spirit is a base, dejected spirit, cross and contrary to the spirit of a Christian, and it is very base.

I remember that the Heathens accounted it very base. Plutarch reports of a certain people, who used to manifest their disdain to men who were overmuch dejected by any affliction, and condemned them to this punishment: to wear women's clothes all their days, or for a certain space of time at least, they should go in women's clothes in token of shame and disgrace to them because they had such effeminate spirits. They thought it against a manly spirit, and therefore, seeing they did un-man themselves, they should go as women. Now, shall they account it an unmanly spirit, to be overmuch dejected in afflictions? and shall not a Christian account it an unchristianlike spirit to be overmuch dejected by any affliction whatsoever? I remember someone else compares murmuring spirits to children, when they are weaning: what a great deal of stir you have with your children when you wean them! how perverse and vexing they are! So, when God would wean you from some outward comforts in this world, oh, how fretting and discontented you are! Children will not sleep themselves nor let their mothers sleep when they are weaning; and so, when God would wean us from the world, and we fret, vex, and murmur, this is a childish spirit.

4. *It is below the profession of a Christian.* The profession of a Christian – what is that? A Christian's profession is to be dead to the world and to be alive to God, that is his profession, to have his life hid with Christ in God, to satisfy himself in God. What! is this your profession? And yet if you have not everything you want, you murmur and are discontented. In that you even deny your profession.

5. *It is below that special grace of faith.* Faith is what overcomes the world; it makes all the promises of God ours. Now when you took upon you the profession of religion did God ever promise you that you would live at ease, and quiet, and have no trouble? I remember Augustine has a similar expression: 'What! is this your faith? Did I ever promise you (he says) that you should flourish in the world? Are you a Chris-

[149]

tian to that end? And is this your faith? I never made any such promise to you when you took upon you to be a Christian.' Oh, it is very contrary to your profession. You have no promise for this, that you should not have such an affliction upon you. And a Christian should live by his faith. It is said that the just live by faith; now you should not look after any other life but the life that you have by faith. You have no ground for your faith to believe that you should be delivered out of such an affliction, and then why should you account it such a great evil to be under this affliction? Certainly the good that we have in the ground for our faith is enough to content our hearts here, and to all eternity.

A Christian should be satisfied with what God has made the object of his faith. The object of his faith is high enough to satisfy his soul, were it capable of a thousand times more than it is. Now if you may have the object of your faith you have enough to content your soul. And know that when you are discontented for want of certain comforts, you should think thus: God never promised me that I should have these comforts, at this time, and in such a way as I would have. I am discontented because I have not these things which God never yet promised me, and therefore I sin much against the Gospel, and against the grace of faith.

6. *It is below a Christian because it is below those helps that a Christian has more than others have.* They have the promises to help them, which others have not. It is not so much for the heart of a Nabal to sink, because he has nothing but the creature to uphold him. But it is much for a Christian, who has promises and ordinances to uphold his spirit, which others have not.

7. *It is below the expectation that God has of Christians,* for God expects not only that they should be patient in afflictions, but that they should rejoice and triumph in them. Now, Christians, when God expects this from you, and you have not even attained to contentedness under afflictions! Oh, this is beneath what God expects from you.

8. *It is below what God has had from other Christians.*

Others have not only been contented with little trials, but they have triumphed under great afflictions, they have suffered the spoiling of their goods with joy. Read the latter part of the eleventh of the Hebrews, and you will find what great things God has had from his people. Therefore not to be content with smaller crosses must needs be a great evil.

9

THE EVILS OF A MURMURING SPIRIT – *concluded*

—————

VI. The sixth evil in a murmuring spirit is, *By murmuring you undo your prayers, for it is exceedingly contrary to the prayers that you make to God.* When you come to pray to God, you acknowledge his sovereignty over you, you come there to profess yourselves to be at God's disposal. What do you pray for, unless you acknowledge that you are at his disposal? Unless you will stand, as it were, at his disposal, never come to petition him. If you will come to petition him and yet will be your own carver you go contrary to your prayers, to come as if you would beg your bread at your Father's gates every day, and yet you must do what you list: this is the undoing of the prayers of a Christian. I remember reading that Latimer, speaking concerning Peter who denied his master, said: 'Peter forgot his Paternoster,* for that was, Hallowed be thy name, and thy kingdom come.' So we may say, when you have murmuring and discontented hearts, you forget your prayers, you forget what you have prayed for. What do you pray, but, Give us this day our daily bread? (For you must make the Lord's prayer a pattern for your prayers; that is Christ's intention, that we should have it as a pattern and a directory, as it were, how to make our prayers.) Now God does not teach any of you to pray, Lord, give me so much a year, or let me have this kind of cloth, and so many dishes at my table. Christ does not teach you to pray so, but he

* Paternoster – The Lord's Prayer, so called because the Latin version begins: 'Pater noster' (Our Father).

teaches us to pray, 'Lord, give us our bread,' showing that you should be content with a little. What, have you not bread to eat? I hope there are none of you here but have that.

Objection. But I do not know what would become of my children if I were to die. Or if I have bread now, I do not know where I shall get it from next week, or where I shall get provision for the winter.

Answer. Where did Christ teach us to pray, Lord, give us provision for so long a time? No, but if we have bread for this day, Christ would have us content. Therefore when we murmur because we have not so much variety as others have, we do, as it were, forget our Paternoster. It is against our prayers; we do not in our lives hold forth the acknowledgement of the sovereignty of God over us as we seem to acknowledge in our prayers. Therefore when at any time you find your hearts murmuring, then do but reflect upon yourselves and think thus: Is this according to my prayers, in which I held forth the sovereign power and authority that God has over me?

VII. The seventh thing which I add for the evil of discontent is *the woeful effects that come to a discontented heart from murmuring.* I will name you five; there are five evil effects that come from a murmuring spirit:

1. *By murmuring and discontent in your hearts, you come to lose a great deal of time.* How many times do men and women, when they are discontented, let their thoughts run, and are musing and contriving, through their present discontentedness and let their discontented thoughts work in them for some hours together, and they spend their time in vain! When you are alone you should spend your time in holy meditation, but you are spending your time in discontented thoughts. You complain that you cannot meditate, you cannot think on good things, but if you begin to think of them a little, soon your thoughts are off from them. But if you are discontented with anything, then you can go alone, and muse, and roll things up and down in your thoughts to feed a discontented humour. Oh, labour to see this evil effect of murmuring, the losing of your time.

2. *It unfits you for duty.* If a man or woman is in a contented frame, you may turn such a one to anything at any time, and he is fit to go to God at any time; but when one is in a discontented condition, then a man or woman is exceedingly unfit for the service of God. And it causes many distractions in duty, it unfits for duty, and when you come to perform duties, oh, the distractions that are in your duties, when your spirits are discontented! When you hear any ill news from sea and cannot bear it, or of any ill from a friend, or any loss or cross, oh, what distractions do they cause in the performance of holy duties! When you should be enjoying communion with God, you are distracted in your thoughts about the trial that has befallen you, whereas had you but a quiet spirit, though great trials befell you, yet they would never hinder you in the performance of any duty.

3. *Consider what wicked risings of heart and resolutions of spirit there are many times in a discontented fit.* In some discontented fits the heart rises against God, and against others and sometimes it even has desperate resolutions what to do to help itself. If the Lord had suffered you to have done what you had sometimes thought to do, in a discontented fit, what wretched misery you would have brought upon yourselves! Oh, it was a mercy of God that stopped you; had not God stopped you, but let you go on when you thought to help yourselves this way and the other way, oh, it would have been ill with you. Do but remember those risings of heart and wicked resolutions that sometimes you have had in a discontented mood, and learn to be humbled for that.

4. *Unthankfulness is an evil and a wicked effect which comes from discontent.* The Scripture ranks unthankfulness among very great sins. Men and women, who are discontented, though they enjoy many mercies from God, yet they are thankful for none of them, for this is the vile nature of discontent, to lessen every mercy of God. It makes those mercies they have from God as nothing to them, because they cannot have what they want. Sometimes it is so even in spiritual things: if they do not have all they desire, the com-

forts that they would have, then what they do have is nothing to them. Do you think that God will take this well? Suppose you were to give a friend or a relation some money to trade with and he came and said: 'What is this you have given me? There are only a few coins here. This is no good to me.' This would be intolerable to you, that he should react to your gift like this, just because you have not given him as much money as he would like. It is just the same when you are ready to say: 'All that God has given me is worthless. It is no good to me. It is only a few coins.' For you to say that what God gives you is nothing and only common gifts, all given in hypocrisy, and counterfeit, when they are the precious graces of God's Spirit and worth more than thousands of worlds – how ungrateful it is! The graces of God's Spirit are nothing to a discontented heart who cannot have all that he would have. And so for outward blessings: God has given you health of body, and strength, and has given you some competence for your family, some way of livelihood, yet because you are disappointed in something that you would have, therefore all is nothing to you. Oh, what unthankfulness is this!

God expects that every day you should spend some time in blessing his name for what mercy he has granted to you. There is not one of you in the lowest condition but you have an abundance of mercies to bless God for, but discontentedness makes them nothing. I remember an excellent saying that Luther has: 'This is the rhetoric of the Spirit of God' he said, 'to extenuate evil things, and to amplify good things: if a cross comes to make the cross but little, but if there is a mercy to make the mercy great.' Thus, if there is a cross, where the Spirit of God prevails in the heart, the man or woman will wonder that it is no greater, and will bless God that though there is such a cross, yet that it is no more: that is the work of the Spirit of God; and if there is a mercy, he wonders at God's goodness, that God granted so great a mercy. The Spirit of God extenuates evils and crosses, and magnifies and amplifies all mercies; and makes all mercies seem to be great, and all afflictions seem to be little. But the Devil goes quite contrary, says Luther, his rhetoric is quite otherwise: he lessens God's mercies, and amplifies evil things. Thus, a godly man wonders at his cross that it is not more, a wicked man wonders his cross is so much: 'Oh', he says, 'none was ever so afflicted as I am.' If there is a cross, the Devil puts the soul to musing on it, and making it greater than it is, and so it brings discontent. And on the other side, if there is a mercy, then it is the rhetoric of the Devil to lessen the mercy. 'Aye, indeed', he says, 'the thing is a good thing, but what is it? It is not a great matter, and for all this, I may be miserable.' Thus the rhetoric of Satan lessens God's mercies, and increases afflictions.

I will give you a striking example of this which we find in Scripture: it is the example of Korah, Dathan and Abiram in Numbers 16. 12, 13: 'And Moses sent to call Dathan, and Abiram, the sons of Eliab: which said, We will not come up: Is it a small thing that thou hast brought us up out of a land that floweth with milk and honey, to kill us in the wilderness, except thou make thyself altogether a prince over us?' Mark, they slighted the land that they were going to, the land of Canaan; that was the land that God promised them should flow with milk and honey. But mark here their discontentedness, because they met with some troubles in the wilderness: oh, it was to slay them, they make their affliction in the wilderness greater than it was, oh, it was to kill them, though indeed it was to carry them to the land of Canaan. But though their deliverance from Egypt was a great mercy, they made it to be nothing, for they say 'You have brought us out of a land that floweth with milk and honey' – what land was that? It was the land of Egypt, the land of their bondage, but they call it a land that flowed with milk and honey, though it was the land of their most cruel and unbearable bondage; whereas they should have blessed God as long as they lived for delivering them out of the land of Egypt. Yet, meeting with some cross they make their deliverance from Egypt no mercy, no, it was rather a misery to them. 'Oh', they say, 'Egypt was a land that flowed with milk and honey.' Oh, what baseness there is in a discontented spirit! A discontented spirit, out of envy to God's grace, will make mercies that are great little, yea to be none at all. Would one ever have thought that such a word could have come from the mouth of an Israelite, who had been under bondage and cried under it? and yet when they meet with a little cross in their way they say, 'You have brought us out of the land that floweth with milk and honey.' To say they were better before than now, and yet before, they could not be contented either: this is the usual, unthankful expression of a discontented heart.

It is so with us now when we meet with any cross in our estates, any taxation and trouble, especially if any among you have been where the enemy have prevailed, you are ready to say: 'We had plenty before, and we are now brought to a condition of hardship, we were better before when we had the Prelates and others to domineer,' and so we are in danger of being brought into that bondage again. Oh, let us take heed of this, of a discontented heart; there is this woeful cursed fruit of discontent, to make men and women unthankful for all the mercies God has granted to them, and this is a sore and grievous evil.

5. Finally, there is this evil effect in murmuring, *it causes shiftings of spirit.* Those who murmur and are discontented are liable to temptations to shift for themselves in sinful and ungodly ways; discontent is the ground of shifting courses and unlawful ways. How many of you are condemned by your consciences of this, that in the time of your afflictions you have sought to shift for yourselves by ways that were sinful against God, and your discontent was the bottom and ground of it? If you would avoid shifting for yourselves by wicked ways, labour to mortify this sin of discontent, to mortify it at the root.

VIII. *There is a great deal of folly, extreme folly, in a discontented heart; it is a foolish sin.* I shall open the folly of it in many respects.

1. *It takes away the present comfort of what you have, because you have not something that you would have.* What a

foolish thing is this, that because I have not got what I want, I will not enjoy the comfort of what I have! Do you not account this folly in your children? : you give them some food and they are not contented, perhaps they say it is not enough, they cry for more, and if you do not immediately give them more they will throw away what they have. Though you account it folly in your children, yet you deal thus with God : God gives you many mercies, but you see others have more mercies than you and therefore you cry for more; but God does not give you what you want and because of that you throw away what you have – is not this folly in your hearts? It is unthankfulness.

2. *By all your discontent you cannot help yourselves, you cannot get anything by it.* Who by taking care can add one cubit to his stature, or make one hair that is white to be black? You may vex and trouble yourselves but you can get nothing by it. Do you think that the Lord will come in mercy a whit the sooner because of the murmuring of your spirits? Oh, no, but mercy will be rather deferred the longer for it; though the Lord was about to send mercy before, yet this disorder of your hearts is enough to put him out of his course of mercy, and though he had thoughts that you should have the thing before, yet now you shall not have it. If you had a mind to give something to your child, yet if you see him in a discontented, fretting mood you will not give it him. And this is the very reason why many mercies are denied to you, because of your discontent. You are discontented for want of them, and therefore you do not get them, you deprive yourselves of the enjoyment of your own desires, because of the discontent of your hearts, because you do not get your desires, and is not this a foolish thing?

3. *There are commonly many foolish attitudes that a discontented heart is guilty of. They carry themselves foolishly towards God and towards men.* Such expressions, and such kinds of behaviour come from them, as to make their friends ashamed of them many times. Their carriages are so unseemly, they are a shame to themselves and their friends.

4. Discontent and murmuring *eats out the good and sweetness of a mercy before it comes*. If God should give a mercy for the want of which we are discontented, yet the blessing of the mercy is, as it were, eaten out before we come to have it. Discontent is like a worm that eats the meat out of the nut, and then when the meat is eaten out of it, you have the shell. If a child were to cry for a nut of which the meat has been eaten out, and is all worm-eaten, what good would the nut be to the child? So you would fain have a certain outward comfort and you are troubled for the want of it, but the very trouble of your spirits is the worm that eats the blessing out of the mercy. Then perhaps God gives it you, but with a curse mixed with it so that you were better not to have it than have it. If God gives the man or woman who is discontented for want of some good thing, that good thing before they are humbled for their discontent, such a man or woman can have no comfort from the mercy, but it will be rather an evil than a good to them. Therefore for my part, if I should have a friend or brother or one who was as dear to me as my own soul, whom I saw discontented for the want of such a comfort, I would rather pray, 'Lord, keep this thing from them, till you shall be pleased to humble their hearts for their discontent; let not them have the mercy till they come to be humbled for their discontent over the want of it, for if they have it before that time they will have it without any blessing.' Therefore it should be your care, when you find your hearts discontented for the want of anything, to be humbled for it, thinking thus with yourselves: Lord, if what I so immoderately desire were to come to me before I am humbled for my discontent for want of it, I am certain I could have no comfort from it, but I should rather have it as an affliction to me.

There are many things which you desire as your lives, and think that you would be happy if you had them, yet when they come you do not find such happiness in them, but they prove to be the greatest crosses and afflictions that you ever had, and on this ground, because your hearts were immoderately set upon them before you had them. As it was with

[159]

Rachel: she must have children or else she died – 'Well', said God, 'seeing you must, you shall have them,' but though she had a child she died according to what she said, 'Give me children or else I die.' So in regard of any other outward comforts, people may have the thing, but oftentimes they have it so as it proves the heaviest cross to them that they ever had in all their lives. The child whom you were discontented for the want of, may have been sick, and your hearts were out of temper for fear that you should lose it; God restores it, but he restores it so as he makes it a cross to your hearts all the days of your lives. Someone observes concerning manna, 'When the people were contented with the allowance that God allowed them, then it was very good, but when they would not be content with God's allowance, but would gather more than God would have them, then, says the text, there were worms in it.' So when we are content with our conditions, and what God disposes of us to be in, there is a blessing in it, then it is sweet to us, but if we must needs have more, and keep it longer than God would have us to have it, then there will be worms in it and it will be no good at all.

5. *It makes our affliction a great deal worse than otherwise it would be.* It in no way removes our afflictions, indeed, while they continue, they are a great deal the worse and heavier, for a discontented heart is a proud heart, and a proud heart will not pull down his sails when there comes a tempest and storm. If a sailor, when a tempest and storm comes, is perverse and refuses to pull down his sails, but is discontented with the storm, is his condition any better because he is discontented and will not pull down his sails? Will this help him? Just so is it, for all the world, with a discontented heart: a discontented heart is a proud heart, and he out of his pride is troubled with his affliction, and is not contented with God's disposal, and so he will not pull down his spirit at all, and make it bow to God in this condition into which God has brought him. Now is his condition any better because he will not pull down his spirit? No, certainly, abundantly worse, it is a thousand to one but that the tempest and storm will overwhelm his soul. Thus you

see what a great deal of folly there is in the sin of discontentment.

IX. *There is a great deal of danger in the sin of discontent, for it highly provokes the wrath of God.* It is a sin that much provokes God against his creature. We find most sad expressions in Scripture, and examples too, how God has been provoked against many for their discontent. In Numbers 14 you have a noteworthy text, and one would think that it was enough for ever to make you fear murmuring: in the 26th verse, it is said, 'The Lord spake unto Moses and unto Aaron, saying' – what did he say? – 'How long shall I bear with this evil congregation, which murmur against me?' How long shall I bear with them? says God, this evil congregation, oh it is an evil congregation that murmur against me, and how long shall I bear with them? They murmur, and they have murmured; as those who have murmuring spirits, and murmuring dispositions, they will murmur again, and again. How long shall I bear with this evil congregation that murmur against me? How justly may God speak this of many of you who are this morning before the Lord: how long shall I bear with this wicked man or woman who murmurs against me, and has usually in the course of their lives murmured against me when anything falls out otherwise than they would have it?

And mark what follows after, 'I have heard the murmurings of the children of Israel.' You murmur, and maybe others do not hear you, it may be that you do not speak at all, or but half-words; yet God hears the language of your murmuring hearts, and those muttering speeches, and those half-words that come from you. And observe further in this verse how the Lord repeats this sin of murmuring, 'How long shall I bear with this evil congregation which murmur against me?' Secondly, 'I have heard their murmuring.' Thirdly, 'which they murmur against me'. Murmur, murmur, murmur – three times in one verse he repeats it, and this is to show his indignation against the thing. When you express indignation against a thing, you repeat it over again, and again; now the Lord, because he would express his indignation against this sin, repeats it over again, and again, and it follows in the 28th verse, 'Say unto them, As truly as I live, saith the Lord, as ye have spoken in mine ears, so will I do to you.' Mark, God swears against a murmurer. Sometimes in your discontent perhaps you will be ready to swear. Do you swear in your discontent? – So does God swear against you for your discontent. And what would God do to them? 'Doubtless your carcases shall fall in the wilderness; and you shall not come into the land concerning which I sware, to make you dwell therein.' It is as if God should say, 'If I have any life in me your lives shall go for it, as I live it shall cost you your lives.' A discontented, murmuring fit of yours may cost you your lives. You see how it provokes God; there is more evil in it than you were aware of. It may cost you your lives, and therefore look to yourselves, and learn to be humbled at the very beginnings of such disorders in the heart. So in Psalm 106. 24, 25: 'Yea, they despised the pleasant land, they believed not his word; but murmured in their tents, and hearkened not unto the voice of the Lord. Therefore he lifted up his hand against them to overthrow them in the wilderness.' There are several things to be observed in this Scripture.

We spoke before of how a murmuring heart slights God's mercies, and so it is here: 'They despised the pleasant land.' And a murmuring heart is contrary to faith: 'they believed not his word, but (says the text) they murmured in their tents, and hearkened not to the voice of the Lord.' Many men and women will hearken to the voice of their own base murmuring hearts, who will not hearken to the voice of the Lord. If you would hearken to the voice of the Lord, there would not be such murmuring as there is. But mark what follows after it; you must not think to please yourselves in your murmuring discontentedness, and think that no evil shall come of it: 'Therefore he lifted up his hand against them to overthrow them.' You who are discontented lift up your hearts against God, and you cause God to lift up his hand against you. Perhaps God lays his finger on you softly in some afflictions, in your families or elsewhere, and you cannot bear the hand of

God, which lies upon you as tenderly as a tender-hearted nurse lays her hand on a child. You cannot bear the tender hand of God which is upon you in a lesser affliction; it would be just for God to lift up his hand against you in another kind of affliction. Oh, a murmuring spirit provokes God exceedingly.

There is another place in 16th of Numbers: compare the 41st verse, and the 46th verse together: 'But on the morrow all the congregation of the children of Israel murmured against Moses and Aaron, saying, Ye have killed the people of the Lord,' and mark in the 46th verse: 'And Moses said unto Aaron, Take a censer and put fire therein from off the altar, and put on incense, and go quickly unto the congregation and make an atonement for them, for there is wrath gone out from the Lord, the plague is begun.' Mark how God's wrath is kindled: in the 41st verse, the congregation had murmured, and they murmured only against Moses and Aaron (perhaps you murmur more directly against God) and that was against God, in murmuring against God's ministers. It was against God but not so directly; if you murmur against those whom God makes instruments, because you have not got everything that you would have, against the Parliament, or such and such who are public instruments, it is against God. It was only against Moses and Aaron that the Israelites murmured, and they said that Moses and Aaron had killed the people of the Lord, though it was the hand of God that was upon them for their former wickedness in murmuring. It is usual for wicked, vile hearts to deal thus with God, when God's hand is a little upon them, to murmur again and again, and so to bring upon themselves infinite kinds of evils. But now the anger of God was quickly kindled: 'Oh', said Moses, 'go, take the censer quickly, for wrath is gone out from Jehovah, the plague is begun.'

So while you are murmuring in your families, the wrath of God may quickly go out against you. In a morning or evening, when you are murmuring, the wrath of God may come quickly upon your families or persons. You are never so prepared for present wrath as when you are in a murmuring, discontented fit. Those who stand by and see you in a murmuring, discontented fit, have cause to say: 'Oh, let us go and take the censer, let us go to prayer, for we are afraid that wrath is gone out against this family, against this person.' And it would be a very good thing for you, who are a godly wife, when you see your husband come home and start murmuring because things are not going according to his desire, to go to prayer, and say: 'Lord, pardon the sin of my husband.' And similarly for a husband to go to God in prayer, falling down and beseeching him that wrath may not come out against his family for the murmuring of his wife. The truth is that at this day there has been, at least lately, as much murmuring in England as there ever was, and even in this very respect the plague has begun. This very judgment comes many times on those who are discontented in their families, and are always grumbling and murmuring at any thing that falls out amiss.

I say this text of Scripture in Numbers clearly holds forth that the Lord brings the plague upon men for this sin of murmuring; he does it in kingdoms and families, and on particular persons. Though we cannot always point out the particular sin that God brings it for, yet we should examine how far we are guilty of the sin of murmuring, because the Scripture holds forth this so clearly, that when Moses but heard that they murmured: 'Do they murmur?' he said, 'go forth quickly and seek to pacify the anger of God, for wrath is gone out, and the plague is begun.' And you have a notable example of God's heavy displeasure against murmuring in 1 Corinthians 10. 10: 'Neither murmur ye as some of them also murmured, and were destroyed of the destroyer.' Take heed of murmuring as some of them did – he speaks of the people of Israel in the wilderness – for, he says, what came of it? They were destroyed of the destroyer. Now the destroyer is thought to be the fiery serpents that were sent among them. They murmured and God sent fiery serpents to sting them. What! do you think that a certain cross and affliction stings you? Perhaps such an affliction is upon you, and it seems to be grievous for the present; what! do you murmur and repine? God has greater crosses to bring upon you. Those people who murmur for the want of outward comforts, for want of water, and for the want of bread, murmur, but the Lord sends fiery serpents among them. I would say to a murmuring heart, 'Woe to you that strive with your maker! Woe to that man, that woman who strives against their maker! What else are you doing but striving against your maker? Your maker has the absolute disposal of you, and will you strive against him? What is this murmuring, discontented heart of yours doing but wrangling and contending and striving even with God himself? Oh, woe to him who strives against his maker! I may further say to you, as God spoke to Job, when he was impatient (Job 38. 1, 2): 'Now God spake', says the text, 'out of the whirlwind, and said, Who is this that darkeneth counsel by words without knowledge?' So, do you speak against God's ways, and his providences which have taken place concerning your condition and outward comforts? Who is this? Who is this that darkeneth counsel by words without knowledge? Where is the man or woman whose heart is so bold and impudent that they dare to speak against the administration of God's providence?

X. *There is a great curse of God upon murmuring and discontent; so far as it prevails in one who is wicked, it has the curse of God upon it.* In Psalm 59. 15, see what the curse of God is upon wicked and ungodly men: 'Let them wander up and down for meat, and grudge if they be not satisfied.' That is the imprecation and curse upon wicked and ungodly men, that if they are not satisfied they shall grudge. When you are not satisfied in your desires and find your heart grudging against God, apply this Scripture – what! is the curse of the wicked upon *me*? This is the curse that is threatened upon wicked and ungodly ones, that they shall grudge if they be not satisfied.

And in Deuteronomy 28. 67, it is threatened as a curse of God upon men that they cannot be content with their present condition: 'But they shall say in the morning, Would God it were even! and at even, Would God it were morning!' So they lie tossing up and down and cannot be content with any condition that they are in, because of the sore afflictions that are upon them. Therefore it is further threatened as a curse upon them, in the 34th verse, that they should be mad for the sight of their eyes which they should see: this is but the extremity of their discontentedness, that is, they shall be so discontented, that they shall even be mad. Many men and women in discontented moods are a mad sort of people, and though you may please yourselves with such a mad kind of behaviour, you should know that it is a curse of God upon men to be given up to a kind of madness for evils which they imagine have come upon them, and which they fear. In the 47th verse, there is a striking expression to show the curse of God on murmuring hearts: The Lord threatens the curses which shall be upon them, and says (verses 45–47): 'The curses shall pursue thee, and they shall be upon thee for a sign, and for a wonder, and upon thy seed for ever: Because thou servedst not the Lord thy God with joyfulness, and with gladness of heart, for the abundance of all things.' God here threatens to bring his curse upon them, so as to make them a wonder and a sign to others. Why? Because they served not the Lord with joyfulness of heart, therefore God would bring such a curse upon them as would make them a wonder to all that were about them. Oh, how far are you, then, who have a murmuring heart, from serving the Lord with joyfulness!

XI. *There is much of the spirit of Satan in a murmuring spirit.* The Devil is the most discontented creature in the world, he is the proudest creature that is, and the most discontented creature, and the most dejected creature. Now, therefore, so much discontent as you have, so much of the spirit of Satan you have. It was the unclean spirit that went up and down and found no rest; so when a man or woman's spirit has no rest, it is a sign that it has much of the unclean spirit, of the spirit of Satan, and you should think with yourself, Oh, Lord, have I the spirit of Satan upon me? Satan is the most discontented spirit that is, and oh! how much of his spirit have I upon me who can find no rest at all!

XII. *If you have a murmuring spirit, you must then have disquiet all the days of your life*. It is as if a man in a great crowd were to complain that other folks touch him. While we are in this world God has so ordered things that afflictions must befall us; and if we will complain and be discontented at every cross and affliction, why, we must complain and be discontented all the days of our lives! Indeed, God in just judgment will let things fall out on purpose to vex those who have vexing spirits and discontented hearts; and therefore it is necessary that they should live disquieted all their days. People will not be troubled much if they upset those who are continually murmuring. Oh, they will have disquiet all their days!

XIII. Finally, there is this further dreadful evil in discontent and murmuring: *God may justly withdraw his care of you, and his protection over you, seeing God cannot please you in his administrations*. We would say so to discontented servants: If you are not pleased, better yourselves when you will. If you have a servant not content with his diet and wages, and work, you say, Better yourselves; so may God justly say to us – we who profess ourselves servants to him, to be in his work, and yet are discontented with this thing or that in God's household, God might justly say – Better yourselves. What if God should say to any of you, If my care over you does not please you, then take care of yourselves, if my protection over you will not please you, then protect yourselves? Now all things that befall you, befall you through a providence of God, and if you are those who belong to God, there is a protection of God over you, and a care of God. If God were to say, 'Well, you shall not have the benefit of my protection any longer, and I will take no further care of you', would not this be a most dreadful judgment of God from Heaven upon you? Take heed what you do then in being discontented with God's will towards you, for, indeed, on account of discontent this may befall you. That is the reason why many people, over whom God's protection has been very gracious for a time, when they have thriven abundantly, yet afterwards almost all who behold them may say of them that they live as if God had cast off his care over them, and as if God did not care what befell them.

Now then, my brethren, put all these points together, those we spoke of in the last chapter, and these points that have been added now in this chapter, for setting out a murmuring and discontented spirit. Oh, what an ugly face has this sin of murmuring and discontentedness! Oh, what cause is there that we should lay our hands upon our hearts, and go away and be humbled before the Lord because of this! Whereas your thoughts were wont to be exercised about providing for yourselves, and getting more comforts for yourselves, let the stream of your thoughts now be turned to humble yourselves for your discontentedness. Oh, that your hearts may break before God, for otherwise you will fall to it again! Oh, the wretchedness of man's heart!

You find in Scripture, concerning the people of Israel, how strangely they fell to their murmuring, again and again. Do but observe three texts of Scripture for that, the first in the 15th of Exodus at the beginning. There you have Moses and the congregation singing to God and blessing God for his mercy: 'Then sang Moses and the children of Israel this song unto the Lord, and spake, saying, I will sing unto the Lord, for he hath triumphed gloriously, the horse and his rider hath he thrown into the sea.' And then: 'The Lord is my strength and song, and he is become my salvation, he is my God and I will prepare him an habitation, my father's God and I will exalt him.' So he goes on: 'and who is like unto thee, O Lord, amongst the gods? who is like thee, glorious in holiness, fearful in praises, doing wonders?' Thus their hearts triumphed in God, but mark, before the chapter is ended, in the 23rd verse: 'When they came to Marah (in the same chapter) they could not drink of the waters of Marah for they were bitter, therefore the name of it was called Marah; and the people murmured against Moses.' After so great a mercy as this, what unthankfulness was there in their murmuring!

Then God gave them water, but in the very next chapter

they fell to their murmuring. You do not read that they were humbled for their former murmuring, and therefore they murmur again (Exodus 16. 1 ff.): 'All the congregation of the children of Israel came to the wilderness of Sin, etc. And the whole congregation' (in the second verse) 'of the children of Israel murmured against Moses and against Aaron in the wilderness, and the children of Israel said unto them, Would to God we had died by the hand of the Lord in the land of Egypt, when we sat by the flesh-pots, and when we did eat bread to the full.' Now they want flesh; they wanted water before, but now they want meat. They fell to murmuring again, they were not humbled for this murmuring against God, not even when God gave them flesh according to their desires, but they fell to murmuring again : they wanted somewhat else. In the very next chapter (they did not go far), in the 17th of Exodus at the beginning : 'And all the congregation of the children of Israel journeyed from the wilderness of Sin and pitched in Rephidim; and there was no water for the people to drink.' Then in the second verse : 'Wherefore the people did chide with Moses, and said, Give us water that we may drink. And Moses said unto them, Why chide ye with me? Wherefore do ye tempt the Lord?' And in the third verse : 'And the people thirsted for water, and the people murmured against Moses and said, Wherefore is this, that thou hast brought us up out of Egypt, to kill us, and our children, and our cattle with thirst?' So one time after another, as soon as ever they had received the mercy, then they were a little quieted, but they were not humbled. I bring these Scriptures to show this, that if we have not been humbled for murmuring, when we meet with the next cross we will fall to murmuring again.

10

AGGRAVATIONS OF THE SIN OF MURMURING

Now because it is very hard to work upon a murmuring spirit, there are many aggravations which we must consider for the further setting out of the greatness of this sin.

I. *To murmur when we enjoy an abundance of mercy; the greater and the more abundant the mercy that we enjoy, the greater and the viler is the sin of murmuring.* For example, when God had newly delivered the people out of the house of bondage, for them to murmur, because they lack some few things that they desire, oh, to sin against God after a great mercy, is a great aggravation, and a most abominable thing. Now, my brethren, the Lord has granted us very great mercies. I will but speak a word of what God has done of late, what mercies has the Lord granted to us this summer, heaped mercies upon us, one mercy upon another! What a condition were we in at the beginning of this summer! And what a different condition are we in now! Oh, what a mercy is it that the Lord has not taken advantage of us, that he has not made those Scriptures before mentioned good upon us for all our murmuring! The Lord has gone on with one mercy after another. We hear of mercy in Bristol, and mercy to our brethren in Scotland. But if after this anything should befall us that is contrary to us, and we should be ready to murmur again at once – Oh, let us not so requite God for those mercies of his! Oh, let us take heed of giving God any ill requital for his mercies! Oh, give God praise according to his excellent greatness, to his excellent goodness and grace!

And now has God given to you the contentment of your hearts? Take heed of being the cause of any grief to your brethren. Do not think that because God has been gracious to you, that therefore he has given you liberty to bring them into bondage. Oh, let not there be such an ill effect of God's mercy to you, as for you for to exclude, by petitioning, or any other way, your brethren whom the Lord has been pleased to make instruments of your peace; let not that be the fruit of it, nor to desire anything that yourselves do not yet understand. God is very jealous of the glory of his mercy, and if any ill use should be made of the mercy of God after we enjoy it, Oh, it would go to the heart of God. Nothing is more grievous to the heart of God than the abuse of mercy, as, for example, if any way that is hard and rigid should be taken towards our brethren, and those especially whom God has made such special instruments of good to us, who have been willing to venture their lives and all for us; if now, when we have our turns served, we let God and his people and servants who helped to save us shift for themselves as well as they can. This is a great aggravation of your sin, to sin against the mercies of God.

For men and women to be discontented in the midst of mercies, in enjoyment of an abundance of mercies, aggravates the sin of discontent and murmuring. To be discontented in any afflicted condition is sinful and evil, but to be discontented when we are in the midst of God's mercies, when we are not able to count the mercies of God, still to be discontented because we have not got all we would have, this is a greater evil. The Lord this summer has multiplied mercies one after another, the Lord has made this summer a continued miracle of mercy. Never did a Kingdom enjoy (in so little a space of time) such mercies one upon another. Now the public mercies of God should quiet our hearts and keep us from discontent. The sin of discontent for private afflictions is exceedingly aggravated by the consideration of public mercies to the land. When the Lord has been so merciful to the land, will you be fretting and murmuring, because you have not in your family all the comforts that you would have?

Just as it is a great aggravation of a man's evil for him to rejoice immoderately in his own private comforts when the Church is in affliction; when the public suffers grievous and hard troubles, if any man shall then rejoice and give liberty to himself, at that time to satisfy his flesh to the uttermost in all outward comforts, this greatly aggravates his sin. So on the contrary for any man to be immoderately troubled for any private afflictions when it goes well with the public, with the Churches, is a great aggravation of his sin. It may be that when the Church of God was lowest, and it went worst in other parts, yet you did abate none of the comforts of your flesh, but gave full liberty to satisfy your flesh as formerly: Know that this was your sin. So, on the other side, when we have received such mercies in public, all our private afflictions should be swallowed up in the public mercies. We should think with ourselves, Though we be afflicted for our part, yet, blessed be God, it goes well with the Church, and with the public interest. Thus the consideration of that should mightily quiet our hearts in all our private discontents, and if it does not do so, know that our sin is much increased by the mercies of God which are abroad. Now shall God's mercies aggravate our sins? This is a sad thing, it is to turn the mercies of God to be our misery. Did you not pray to God for these mercies which God sent of late to the public? these great victories that God has given, did you not pray for them? Now you have them, is not there enough in them to quiet your heart for some private trouble you meet with in your family? Is not there goodness enough there to cure your discontent? Certainly, such mercies were not so worthy to be prayed for, except they have so much excellence in them as to countervail some private afflictions.

Public mercies are the aggravation of private discontent. It is so of public discontent too: if we receive so many public mercies, and yet if every thing goes not in the public according as we desire, we are discontented at that, it will greatly aggravate our sin. God may say, 'What! shall I bestow such mercies upon a people, and yet, if they have not everything they would have, they will be discontented?' Oh, it is exceedingly evil. So in particular, with the mercies that concern yourself, your family: if you would consider, you have many more mercies than afflictions – I dare boldly aver it concerning anyone in this congregation. Let your afflictions be what they will, there is not one of you, but has more mercies than afflictions.

Objection. You will say, Yes, but you do not know what our afflictions are; our afflictions are such as you do not conceive of, because you do not feel them.

Answer. Though I cannot know what your afflictions are, yet I know what your mercies are, and I know they are so great that I am sure there can be no afflictions in this world as great as the mercies you have. If it were only this mercy, that you have this day of grace and salvation continued to you: it is a greater mercy than any affliction. Set any affliction beside this mercy and see which would weigh heaviest; this is certainly greater than any affliction. That you have the day of grace and salvation, that you are not now in hell, this is a greater mercy. That you have the sound of the Gospel still in your ears, that you have the use of your reason: this is a greater mercy than your afflictions. That you have the use of your limbs, your senses, that you have the health of your bodies; health of body is a greater mercy than poverty is an affliction. No man who is rich, if he is wise, and has a sickly body, would not part with all his riches that he might have his health. Therefore your mercies are more than your afflictions.

We find in Scripture how the Holy Ghost aggravates the sin of discontent from the consideration of mercies: you have a notable Scripture for this in the 16th of Numbers, verse 8 and following. It is a speech of Moses to Korah and his company, when they murmured: 'And Moses said unto Korah, Hear, I pray you, ye sons of Levi' (that is something, that you are sons of Levi), 'Seemeth it but a small thing unto you that the God of Israel hath separated you from the congregation of Israel, to bring you near to himself to do the service of the tabernacle of the Lord, and to stand before the congregation to minister unto them?' Korah and his company were murmuring, but mark how Moses aggravates this: 'Seemeth it a small thing unto you that the God of Israel hath separated you from the congregation of Israel to bring you near to himself to do the service of the tabernacle of the Lord? etc.' You see, it is a great honour that God puts upon a man, a great mercy that he bestows upon any man, to separate him from others for himself, to come near to him, to employ him in the service of the tabernacle, to minister to the congregation in holy things. This is a great mercy, and, indeed, it is such a mercy that one would think there should be none upon whom God bestows such a mercy who would have a murmuring heart for any affliction. It is true, many ministers of God meet with hard things which might discourage them, and trouble and grieve their spirits; but this consideration, that God is pleased to employ them in such a service near to himself, that though they cannot do good to themselves, yet they may do good to others, this should quiet them. And yet in the 10th verse: 'And he hath brought thee near to him, and all thy brethren the sons of Levi with thee, and seek ye the priesthood also?' Have you not enough already? But still you are discontented with what you have, and must have more; do you seek still more? 'Seek ye the priesthood also? For which cause both thou and all thy company are gathered together against the Lord: and what is Aaron, that ye murmur against him?' What, has God given you such things, and yet will you be murmuring, because you cannot have more? Methinks that this place should keep ministers from murmuring, no matter what afflictions and crosses, and unkind dealings they meet with from men, yet still they should go on with hearts quiet and discomforted in the work that God has set them about, and labour to countervail all their afflictions by being more abundant in the work of the Lord. That is the first text of Scripture that shows how the mercies we enjoy are aggravations of the sin of murmuring

Then a second Scripture is in the 2nd of Job, verse 10. It is a speech of Job to his wife: What? said Job, when his wife would have him curse God and die, which was a degree beyond murmuring, Why, he said, 'thou speakest as one of the foolish women. Shall we receive good at the hand of God and not evil?' You see, Job helped himself against all murmuring thoughts against the ways of God, with this consideration, that he had received so much good from the Lord. What though we receive evil, yet do we not receive good as well as evil? Let us set one against the other: that is the way we should go. In the 7th of Ecclesiastes, the 14th verse, you find a notable Scripture whereby you may see what course is to be taken when the heart rises in murmuring: 'In the day of prosperity be joyful, but in the day of adversity consider.' What should they consider? Mark what follows: 'God also hath set the one over against the other, to the end that man should find nothing after him.' 'God also hath set the one over against the other,' thus, when you are in prosperity, then indeed every man can be joyful, but what if afflictions befall you, what then? Then consider – consider what? 'That God hath set one over against the other'; you have a great deal of affliction, and you have had a great deal of prosperity, you have many troubles, and you have had many mercies: make one column of mercies, and one column of afflictions, and write one against the other, and see if God has not filled one column as full as the other. You look altogether upon your afflictions, but look upon your mercies also.

For instance, it may be God has afflicted you in one child, but he has been merciful to you in another child: set one against the other. God afflicted David in Absalom, but he was merciful to David in Solomon, and, therefore, when David cried out: 'Oh Absalom, my son, my son,' if he had thought of Solomon, and cried, 'Oh Solomon, my son, my son,' it would have quieted him. And it may be God has been merciful to you in a wife, or in your husband: set that against your affliction. It may be, God crosses you in your possessions, but that he employs you in his service. It may be, you are afflicted in some of your friends, but you have other friends who are great mercies to you, and therefore you should set one against the other; and it concerns you to do so, for those mercies will be aggravations of your sins, and you had better make God's mercies a means to lessen your sins, than to be the aggravation of your sins. If you do not make the mercies of God help you against your murmuring, you will make them aggravations of the sin of murmuring.

Take but this one further consideration, and if you will but work it on your hearts, I hope you may find a great deal of power in it. You find afflictions, and your hearts are troubled and murmur; consider how God's mercies aggravate this sin. In the midst of our sins we reckon that God should accept our services. Do but consider thus : if in the midst of our many sins we hope that God will accept our poor services, why, then, should we not in the midst of our afflictions bless God for his many mercies? Shall God be thus gracious to us that, notwithstanding our many sins, yet he will not cast away our poor duties and services that we perform? then why should not we in the midst of our sufferings accept what mercies we have, and not slight them and disregard them? If you, in the midst of God's mercies, are not willing to bear the afflictions that God lays upon you, then it is just with God that, in the midst of your sins, he should not regard any of your duties. Now is there not as much power in your manifold sins to cause God to reject your duties and services, as there is power in afflictions (in the midst of many mercies) to take off your heart from being affected with God's mercies? And that is the first aggravation of the sin of murmuring, to murmur in the midst of mercies.

II. A second aggravation of the sin of murmuring is, *When we murmur for small things.* Naaman's servant said to him, Father (for so he called him), if the prophet had required you to do some great thing, would not you have done it? How much more this little thing. So I say, if the Lord had required you to suffer some great thing, would not you have been willing to suffer? How much more this little thing! I remember reading in Seneca a Heathen, that he has this comparison which is a very fine one to set out the great evil of murmuring over smaller afflictions: he says, Suppose a man has a very fine house to dwell in, and he has beautiful orchards and gardens, set about with handsome tall trees for ornament. If this man should now murmur because the wind blows a few leaves off his trees, what a most unreasonable thing it would be, for him to be weeping, and wringing his hands over the loss of a few leaves, when he has plenty of all kinds of fruit? Thus it is with many, says Seneca, though they have a great many comforts about them, yet some little thing, the blowing off of a few leaves from them is enough to disquiet them. It was a great evil that when Ahab had a kingdom, the lack of his neighbour's vineyard had such power to disquiet him. So for us to murmur, not because we have not got such a thing as we have need of, but because we have not got what possibly we might have: this is a very great sin.

Suppose God gives a woman a child who has all his limbs and parts complete, a child who is very comely, with excellent gifts, wit and memory, but maybe there is a wart growing on the finger of the child, and she murmurs at it, and, Oh, what an affliction this is to her! She is so taken up with it, that she forgets to give any thanks to God for her child, and all the goodness of God to her in the child is swallowed up in that. Would you not say that this was folly and a very great evil in a woman to do so? Truly, our afflictions, if we weighed them aright, are but such things in comparison of our mercies Rebekah had a mighty desire to have children, but because she found some trouble in her body when she was with child, said, 'Why am I thus?' As if she should say, I had rather have none, only because she found a little pain and trouble in her body. To be discontented when the affliction is small and little that increases very much the sin of murmuring. It is too much for anyone to murmur over the heaviest cross that can befall one in this world, but to be discontented and murmur over some small things, that is worse. I have read of someone who when he lay upon a heap of damask-roses, complained that one of the rose leaves lay double under him. So we are ready thus for very small things to make complaints, and to be discontented with our condition, and that is a second aggravation.

III. *For men of gifts and abilities to whom God has given wisdom, to be discontented and murmur, is more than if others do it.* Murmuring and discontentedness is too much in the weakest, yet we can bear with it sometimes in children and women who are weak, but for those who are men, men of understanding, who have wisdom, whom God employs in public service, that they should be discontented with everything, is an exceedingly great evil. For men, to whom God has given gifts and wisdom, when things fall out amiss in their families, to be always murmuring and repining, is a greater sin than for women or children to do it.

IV. *The consideration of the freeness of all God's mercies to us.* Whatever we have is free of cost. What though we have not got all we would have, seeing what we have is free! If what we have were earned then it would be something, but when we consider that all is from God, for us to murmur at his dispensations is very evil. Suppose a man were entertained in a friend's family, and did not pay for his board, but had it given him for nothing: you would not expect him to be ready to find fault with everything in the house, with servants, or with the meat at table, or the like. If such a one who has plentiful provision and all given him gratis, and pays nothing for his board, should be discontented when a cup is not filled for him as he would have it, or when he has to wait a minute longer for a thing than he would, we would reckon this a great evil. So it is with us: we are at God's table every day, and it is free, whatever we have. It is accounted very unmannerly for a man at his friend's table to find fault with things, though at home he may be outspoken. Now when we are at the table of God (for all God's administrations to us are his table) and are free from lusts, for us to be finding fault and to be discontented is a great aggravation of our sin.

V. *For men and women to murmur and be discontented and impatient, when they have the things for the want of which they were discontented before.* So it is sometimes with children: they will cry for a thing, and when you give it them, then throw it away; they are as much discontented as they were before. So it was with the people of Israel, nothing would quiet them but they must have a king. Samuel would have persuaded them to the contrary, and told them what kind of king they would have. And when they had a king: 'What shall a king do to us?' (Hosea 10. 3); they were not contented when they had one. So Rachel must have children or else she died, and when she had a little trouble she was discontented too. So that, as we say, we are not well, either full or fasting.

VI. *For those men and women to be discontented and murmur whom God has raised from mean and low estates and positions.* This is a very great aggravation, if you are discontented now. There was a time when you were low enough, and perhaps when you were so low then you said, 'Oh, if God would deliver me from such an affliction, or give me but a little more wealth, I should think myself in a good condition.' But if God by his providence does raise you, you are still as greedy of more as you were before, and as much discontented as you were before. It is an evil thing for people who had mean breeding, and poor beginnings to be so fastidious that nothing can please them, whereas there was a time not long since when they were low and mean enough. But it is very common for those who are raised from a low and mean condition to be more nice and dainty and more proud when they are raised than others who are of better breeding.

It is too much for a child to be discontented in his father's house, but if you have taken a poor beggar boy, who lay begging at your door, into your house, and set him at your own table, could you bear that he should complain that some dish is not well dressed, or the like? You could not bear it if your children should do it, but you could bear it a great deal better from them than to hear such a one do it. But you are a poor beggar, and God has, as it were, taken you into his great family, and if the Lord has been pleased to raise you higher, so that now you have a competence, that you may live as a man, to be of use and service in the place where God has set you: now will you be discontented because you have not everything that you desire? We know that when the prodigal came to himself, he said, 'In my father's house is bread enough'; he did not say, 'There is good cheer enough and a great deal of dainties.' No, he thought of nothing but bread, 'There is bread enough.' So it is common for men and women, when they are in a low condition, to think that if they may have bread and any competence, they will be contented and bless God; but when they have their bread and things convenient, then they must have more or else they are not contented. Know that this is an exceedingly great aggravation to your discontent, when you are raised from a very low condition, and yet you cannot be contented with what you have.

VII. *For those to be discontented who have been very great sinners and ungodly in their former life.* For men and women who have much guiltiness upon them, the guilt of very many sins upon them, who have provoked God exceedingly against them, and have brought themselves in a most dreadful manner under the sentence of God's justice, and yet, God having been pleased to reprieve them – for them to murmur and to be discontented with God's administrations towards them is exceedingly evil. Oh, it were consideration enough to quiet any murmuring in our hearts, to think thus, We are but sinners, why should we not be sufferers who are sinners? But then consider, we who are such great sinners, guilty of such notorious sins that it is a wonder that we are out of Hell at the present, yet for us to be discontented and murmur, how exceedingly this increases our sin! Consider how we have crossed God in our sins; then if God should cross us in the way of our sufferings, should not we sit down quiet without murmuring? Certainly you never knew what it was to be humbled for your manifold sins, who are discontented at any administration of God towards you!

VIII. *For men who are of little use in the world to be discontented.* If you have a beast that you make much use of, you will feed it well, but if you have but little use of him then

[180]

you turn him into the commons;* little provision serves his turn because you do not make use of him. If we lived so as to be exceedingly useful to God and his Church, we might expect that God would be pleased to come in some encouraging way to us, but when our consciences tell us we live and do but little service for God, why, what if God should turn us upon the commons? We are being fed according to our work. Why should any creature be serviceable to you, who are so little serviceable to God? To meditate on this alone would much help us – to think: I am discontented because such and such creatures are not serviceable to me, but why should I expect them to be serviceable to me, when I am not serviceable to God? That is the eighth aggravation.

IX. *For us to be discontented at a time when God is about to humble us.* It should be the care of a Christian to observe what are God's ways towards him: What is God about to do with me at this time? Is God about to raise me, to comfort me? Let me accept God's goodness, and bless his name; let me join with the work of God, when he offers mercy to me, to take the mercy he offers. But again, is God about to humble me? Is God about to break my heart, and to bring my heart down to him? Let me join with God in this work of his: this is how a Christian should walk with God. It is said that Enoch and Noah walked with God – walked with God, what is that? It is, To observe what work God is now about, and to join with God in that work of his; so that, according as God turns this way or that way, the heart should turn with God, and have workings suitable to the workings of God towards him.

Now I am discontented and murmuring, because I am afflicted; but that is why you are afflicted, because God would humble you. The great design God has in afflicting you, is to break and humble your heart; and will you maintain a spirit quite opposite to the work of God? For you to murmur and be discontented is to resist the work of God. God is doing you good if you could see it, and if he is pleased to sanctify your affliction to break that hard heart of yours, and humble that

* Common grazing-ground.

[181]

proud spirit of yours, it would be the greatest mercy that you ever had in all your life. Now will you still stand out against God? It is just as if you were to say, 'Well, the Lord is about to break me, and humble me, but he shall not': this is the language of your murmuring and your discontentedness, though you dare not say so. But though you do not say so in words, yet it is certainly the language of the temper of your spirit. Oh, consider what an aggravation this is: I am discontented when God is about to work such a work upon me as is for my good; yet I stand out against him and resist him. That is another aggravation.

X. *The more palpable and remarkable the hand of God appears to bring about an affliction, the greater is the sin of murmuring and discontent under an affliction.* It is a great evil at any time to murmur and be discontented, but though it is a sin, when I see an ordinary providence working for me, not to submit to it, when I see an extraordinary providence working, that is a greater sin. That is to say, when I see the Lord working in some remarkable way about an affliction beyond what anyone could have thought of, shall I resist such a remarkable hand of God? shall I stand out against God, when I see he expresses his will in such a remarkable manner that he would have me to be in such a condition? Indeed, before the will of God is apparent, we may desire to avoid an affliction, and may use means for it, but when we see God expressing his will from heaven in a manner beyond what is ordinary and more remarkable, then certainly it is right for us to fall down and submit to him, and not to oppose God when he comes with a mighty stream against us. It is our best way to fall down before him and not to resist, for just as it is an argument of a man's disobedience, when there is not only a command against a sin but when God reveals his command in a terrible way— the more solemn the command of God is, the greater is the sin in breaking that command—so the more remarkable the hand of God is in bringing an affliction upon us, the greater is our sin in murmuring and being discontented. God expects us to fall down when he, as it were, speaks from Heaven to us by name and says, 'Well, I will have this spirit of yours down. Do you not see that my hand is stretched out, my eyes are upon you, my thoughts are upon you, and I must have that proud spirit of yours down?' Oh, then, it is fitting for the creature to yield and submit to him. When you speak in an ordinary manner to your servants or children, you expect them to regard what you say, but when you make them stand still by you, and speak to them in a more solemn way, then if they should disregard what you say, you are very impatient. So, certainly, God cannot take it well whenever he appears from Heaven in such a remarkable way to bring an affliction, if then we do not submit to him.

XI. *To be discontented though God has been exercising us for a long time under afflictions, yet still to remain discontented.* For a man or woman when an affliction first befalls them, to have a murmuring heart, is an evil, but to have a murmuring heart when God has been a long time exercising them with affliction is more evil. Though a heifer when the yoke is first put upon her wriggles up and down and will not be quiet, if after many months or years it will not draw quietly, the husbandman would rather fatten it and prepare it for the butcher than be troubled any longer with it. So though the Lord was content to pass by that discontented spirit of yours at first, yet now that God has for a long time kept the yoke on you – you have been under his afflicting hand, it may be, many years, and yet you remain discontented still – it would be just if God were to bear your murmuring no longer, and that your discontent under the affliction were but a preparation for your destruction.

So, you see, when a man or woman has been long exercised with afflictions, and is still discontented, that is an aggravation of the sin. Mark that text in Hebrews 12. 11: 'Now', says the Scripture, 'no chastening for the present is joyous, but grievous, nevertheless afterward it yieldeth the peaceable fruit of righteousness unto them which are exercised thereby.' It is true our afflictions are not joyous, but grievous. Though at first when our affliction comes it is very grievous, afterwards, says the text, it yieldeth the peaceable fruit of righteousness to those that are exercised thereby. When you have been a long time in the school of afflictions, you are a very dullard in Christ's school if you have not learned this contentment. 'I have learned', said St. Paul, 'in every estate therewith to be content.' Paul had learned this lesson quickly; you have been learning many years. Perhaps you may say, as Heman did, that you are afflicted from your youth up (Psalm 88). Oh, it is a very evil thing if, having been exercised long with afflictions, you are not yet contented. The eye in a man's body is as tender as any part of his body, but yet the eye is able to continue in and bear a great deal of cold, because it is more used to it. So those who are used to afflictions, those whom God exercises much with afflictions (though they have tender spirits otherwise) yet they should have learned contentedness by this time. A new cart may creak and make a noise, but after it has been used a while it will not do so. So when you are first a Christian and newly come into the work of Christ, perhaps you make a noise and cannot bear affliction; but are you an old Christian and yet will you be a murmuring Christian? Oh, it is a shame for any who are old believers, who have been a long time in the school of Jesus Christ, to have murmuring and discontented spirits.

I I

THE EXCUSES OF A DISCONTENTED HEART

But now, my brethren, because this discontented humour is tough, and very hard to work upon – there is none who is discontented but has something to say for their discontent – I shall therefore seek to take away what every discontented heart has to say for himself.

I. *One that is discontented says, 'It is not discontent; it is a sense of my condition.'* I hope you would have me sensible of my condition. Perhaps when God takes away a friend or some other comfort, they are inordinately sorrowful, and wringing their hands as if they were undone; but let anyone speak to them, and they say, 'Would you not have me sensible of my affliction?' Thus many would hide their sinful murmuring under God's hand with this pretence, that it is but sensibleness of their affliction. To that I answer:

1. There is no sense of any affliction that will hinder the sense of God's mercies. Nay, the more we are sensible of our afflictions, providing it is in a gracious manner, the more sensible we will be of God's mercy. But you are so sensible of your affliction that it takes away the sense of all your mercies. Oh, this is sinful discontent, this is not to be sensible of your condition as God would have you, but it is to be sensible in a wicked way, you go beyond your bounds. By this rule you may come to know when your sorrows and troubles for your afflictions go beyond the bounds. We may be sorrowful when God afflicts, but, oh, that I might know when my sorrow goes beyond the bounds of it! Truly, you may know it by this,

does the sense of your afflictions take away the sense of your mercies? If it does, then it goes beyond the bounds.

2. If it were but a bare sense of an affliction it would not hinder you in the duties of your condition. The right sense of our afflictions will never hinder us in the performance of the duties of our condition; but you are so sensible of the affliction that you are made unfit for the performance of the duties of the condition that God has put you in. Surely it is more than mere sense of your affliction!

3. If it were but a mere sense of your affliction, then you could in this your condition bless God for the mercies that others have; but your discontentedness usually breeds envy at others. When anyone is discontented with their condition, they have an envious spirit at the conditions of those who are delivered from what afflictions they bear. Certainly, then, it has turned sour when you are so sensible of your afflictions and insensible of mercies that you are unfit for the duties of your condition, and envious of others who are not afflicted as you are.

II. But a discontented heart will say, *'I am not so much troubled with my afflictions, but it is for my sin rather than my affliction, and I hope you will give leave that we should be troubled and discontented with our sin.* Were it not for sin that I see in myself, I should not be so discontented as I am. Oh! it is sin that is heavy upon me, and it is that which troubles me more than my afflictions.

Do not deceive your own heart, there is a very great deceit in this. There are many people who, when God's hand is out against them, will say they are troubled for their sin, but the truth is, it is the affliction that troubles them rather than their sin. Their heart greatly deceives them in this very thing.

1. They were never troubled for their sin before this affliction came. But you will say, It is true I was not before, for my prosperity blinded me, but now God has opened my eyes by afflictions. Has he? Then your great care will be rather for the removing of your sin than your affliction. Are you more

solicitous about the taking away of your sin than the taking away of your affliction?

2. If it is your sin that troubles you, then even if God should take away your afflictions, yet unless your sin is taken away, and your heart is better, this would not content you, you could not be satisfied. But we see usually that if God removes their afflictions, they have no more trouble for their sin. Oh, many deceive themselves in this, saying that they are so troubled for their sin, and especially those who are so troubled that they are in danger to miscarry, and to make away with themselves. There is not one in ten thousand who is in such a condition as this, and it is afflictions rather than sin that puts them to it. Indeed, you lay everything on this, as if it were the work of the Word, or the spirit of bondage. I remember I heard not long since of a divine who was judicious, and used to such things, to whom came a man mightily troubled for his sin, and he could not tell what to do, he was ready to despair. The divine looked upon him, and said, 'Are you not in debt?' He confessed that he was, and at length the minister began to find out that that was his trouble rather than his sin, and so was able to help him in that matter, that his creditors should not come on him, and then the man was pretty quiet, and would not do away with himself any longer.

It is usual that if anything befalls a man which crosses him, Oh, then, it is his sin that troubles him! Sometimes it is so with servants, if their masters cross them, then they are vexed and fret. Come to deal with them, Oh, then they will say they are sorrowful for their sin. But we must take heed of dallying with God, who is the seer and searcher of the secrets of all hearts. Many of you go sullen and dumpish up and down in your homes, and then you say, it is your sin that lies upon you, when God knows it is otherwise: it is because you cannot have your desires as you would have.

3. If you are troubled for your sin, then it will be your great care not to sin in your trouble, so as not, by your trouble, to increase your sin. But you are troubled in such a

way that, the truth is, you increase your sin in your trouble, and since you said you were troubled for your sin you have committed more sin than you did before.

4. And then, lastly, if it is your sin that troubles you, then you have the more need to submit to God's hand, and to accept the punishment of your iniquity, as in Leviticus 26. 41. There is no consideration to take away murmuring, so much as to look upon my sin as the cause of my affliction.

III. 'Oh', says another, 'I find my affliction is such that God withdraws himself from me in my affliction. That is what troubles me, and can anybody be quiet then, can anybody be satisfied with such a condition, when the Lord withdraws himself? However great my affliction were, yet if I found not God withdrawing himself from me, I hope I could be content with any affliction, but I cannot find the presence of God with me in this affliction, as at other times I have found, and that is what troubles me, and makes me in such a condition as I am.' Now to that I answer thus:

1. It is a very evil thing for men and women over every affliction to conclude that God is departed from them. It may be, when it comes to be examined, there is no other reason why you think that God is withdrawn and departed, but because he afflicts you. Now for you to make such a conclusion, that every time God lays an affliction upon you, he is departed, is a sinful disorder of your heart, and is very dishonourable to God, and grievous to his Spirit. In the 17th of Exodus, verse 7, you may see how God was displeased with such a disorder as this: 'And he called the name of the place Massah, and Meribah, because of the chiding of the children of Israel, and because they tempted the Lord, saying, Is the Lord among us or not?' Mark, they murmured because they were brought into afflictions; but see what the text says, 'Therefore the place was called Massah and Meribah, because they tempted the Lord, saying, Is the Lord among us or not?' This was tempting God. Sometimes we are afraid God is departed from us, and it is merely because we are afflicted. I beseech you to observe this Scripture: God calls it a tempting

[188]

of him, when he afflicts anyone, for them to conclude and say that God is departed from them. If a child should cry out and say that his father is turned to be an enemy to him, because he corrects him, this would be taken ill. I beseech you consider this one place – it may be of very great use to you – that you may not be ready to think that God is departed, because you are afflicted.

2. If God is departed, the greatest sign of God's departing is because you are so disturbed. You make your disquiet the fruit of God's departing, and if it is examined, your disquiet is the cause of God's departing from you. If you could only cure your disquiet, if you could but quiet your own hearts and get them into a better frame of contentedness under God's hand in affliction, then you would find God's presence with you. Will you be thus disquieted till God comes again to you? Your disquiet drives him from you, and you can never expect God's coming to manifest himself comfortably to your souls, till you have gotten your hearts quiet under your afflictions. Therefore you see here how you reason amiss: you reason, I am disquiet because God is gone, when the truth is, God is gone because you are disquiet. Reason the other way, Oh, my disquiet has driven God from me, and therefore if ever I would have the presence of God to come again to me, let my heart be quiet under the hand of God.

3. Do you find God departing from you in your affliction? Will you therefore depart from God too? Is this your help? Can you help yourself that way? Because God is gone, will you go too? Do I, indeed, feel God departing from me? It may be so. It may be, God for your trial is departed a little from you. And is it so indeed? What an unwise course I take! I commit further sin and so I go further off from God; what a plight I am in! God goes from me, and I from God. If the child sees the mother going from it, it is not for the child to say, My mother is gone yonder and I will go the other way; no, but the child goes crying after the mother. So should the soul say, I see the Lord is withdrawing his presence from me, and now it is best for me to make after the Lord with all my

might, and I am sure this murmuring humour is not a making after God, but by it I go further and further away from God, and what a distance there will be between God and me within a little while!

These are some of the reasonings and pleas of a murmuring and discontented heart. There are many others that we shall meet with, and endeavour to speak to your hearts in them, that this tough humour of discontent may, as it were, be cut with the word and softened with the word, so that it may pass away. For that is the way of physicians, when they meet with a body which has any tough humour, then they give that which has a piercing quality; when there is a tough humour which stops the water, that it cannot pass, they give something with a piercing quality which may make a passage for it. So you have need of such things as are piercing, to make a way through this tough humour in the spirits of men and women, whereby they come to live very uncomfortably to themselves and others, and very dishonourably unto God.

Now many pleas and reasonings still remain, for there is a great deal of ado with a discontented, murmuring heart. And I remember, I find that the same Hebrew word which signifies *to lodge, to abide*, signifies *to murmur*. They use one word for both, for murmuring is a disorder that lodges in men; where it gets in once it lodges, abides and continues, and therefore, that we may dislodge it and get it out, we will labour to show what are the further reasonings of a discontented heart.

IV. *'I think I could be content with God's hand,'* says one, *'so far as I see the hand of God in a thing I can be content. But when men deal so unreasonably and unjustly with me, I do not know how to bear it. I can bear that I should be in God's hands, but not in the hands of men. When my friends or acquaintances deal so unrighteously with me, oh, this goes very hard with me, so that I do not know how to bear it from men.'* For taking away this reasoning, consider:

1. Though they are men who bring this cross on you, yet they are God's instruments. God has a hand in it, and they can go no further than God would have them go. This was what

quieted David when Shimei cursed him: God has a hand in it, he said, though Shimei is a base, wicked man, yet I look beyond him to God. So, do any of your friends deal injuriously with you, and wrongly with you? Look up to God, and see that man but as an instrument in God's hands.

2. If this is your trouble that men do so wrong you, you ought rather to turn your hearts to pity them, than to murmur or be discontented. For the truth is, if you are wronged by other men, you have the better of it, for it is better to bear wrong than to do wrong a great deal. If they wrong you, you are in a better condition than they, because it is better to bear, than to do wrong. I remember it is said of Socrates that, as he was very patient when wrong was done to him, they asked him how he came to be so. He said, 'If I meet a man in the street who is a diseased man, shall I be vexed and fretted with him because he is diseased? Those who wrong me I look upon as diseased men, and therefore pity them.'

3. Though you meet with hard dealings from men, yet you meet with nothing but kind, good and righteous dealings from God. When you meet with unrighteous dealings from them, set one against the other. And that is an answer to the fourth plea.

V. 'Oh, but the affliction that comes upon me is an affliction which I never looked for. I never thought I would meet with such an affliction, and that is what I cannot bear. That is what makes my heart so disturbed because it was altogether unlooked for and unexpected.' For the answer of this:

1. It is your weakness and folly that you did not look for it and expect it. In Acts 20. 22, 23, see what St. Paul says concerning himself, 'And now, behold, I go bound in the spirit unto Jerusalem, not knowing the things that shall befall me there, save that the Holy Ghost witnesseth in every city, saying that bonds and afflictions abide me.' It is true, he says, I do not know the particular affliction that may befall me, but this I know, that the Spirit of God witnesses that bonds and afflictions shall abide me everywhere. I look for nothing else but bonds and afflictions wheresoever I go. So a Christian

should do: he should look for afflictions wheresoever he is, in all conditions he should look to meet with afflictions; and therefore if any affliction should befall him, though indeed he could not foresee the particular evil, yet he should think, This is no more than I looked for in general. Therefore no affliction should come unexpectedly to a Christian.

2. A second answer I would give is this: Is it unexpected? Then the less provision you made for it before it came, the more careful should you be to sanctify God's name in it, now it is come. It is in this case of afflictions as in mercies: many times mercy comes unexpected, and that might be a third answer to you. Set one against the other. I have many mercies that I never looked for, as well as afflictions that I never looked for; why should not the one rejoice me as much as the other disturbs me? As it is in mercies, when they come unexpected, the less preparation there was in me for receiving mercy, the more need I have to be careful now to give God the glory of the mercy, and to sanctify God's name in the enjoyment of the mercy. Oh, so it should be with us now: we have had mercies this summer that we never expected, and therefore we were not prepared for them; now we should be so much the more careful to give God the glory of them. So when afflictions come that we did not expect, when it seems we did not lay in for them beforehand, we had need be the more careful to sanctify God's name in them. We should have spent some pains before, to prepare for afflictions and we did not; then take so much the more pains to sanctify God in this affliction now.

VI. 'Oh, but it is very great, my affliction is exceeding great,' says someone, 'and however you say we must be contented, you may say so who do not feel such great afflictions, but if you felt my affliction, which I feel, you would think it hard to bear and be content.' To that I answer:

1. Let it be as great an affliction as it will, it is not as great as your sin. He has punished you less than your sins.

2. It might have been a great deal more, you might have been in Hell. And it is, if I remember, Bernard's saying: he

said, 'It is an easier matter to be oppressed than to perish.' You might have been in Hell, and therefore the greatness of the thing should not make you murmur, even grant it to be great.

3. It may be it is the greater because your heart murmurs so. Shackles upon a man's legs, if his legs are sore, will pain him more. If the shoulder is sore, the burden is the greater. It is because your heart is so unsound that your affliction is great to you.

VII. *But however you may lessen my affliction, yet I am sure it is far greater than the affliction of others.*

1. It may be it is your discontent that makes it greater, when indeed it is not so in itself.

2. If it were greater than others', why is your eye evil because the eye of God is good? Why should you be discontented the more because God is gracious to others?

3. Is your affliction greater than others'? Then in this you have an opportunity to honour God more than others. You should consider, does God afflict me more than other men? God gives me an opportunity in this to honour him in this affliction more than other men, to exercise more grace than other men. Let me labour to do it then.

4. If all afflictions were laid upon a heap together – this is a notable saying of Solon, that wise Heathen, he said – 'Suppose all the afflictions that are in the world were laid upon a heap, and every man should come and take a proportion of those afflictions, every one equally, there is scarce any man but would rather say, Let me have the afflictions that I had before, or else he would be likely to come to a greater share, a greater affliction if so be he should equally share with all the world.' Now for you who are poor (who are not in extremity of poverty), if all the riches in the world were laid together and you should have an equal share, you would be poorer. But take all afflictions and sorrows whatsoever; if all the sorrows in the world were laid together in a heap, and you had but an equal share of them, your portion would be rather more than it is now for the present. And therefore do not

complain that it is more than others', and murmur because of that.

VIII. Another reasoning that murmuring hearts have is this: *Why, they think that if the affliction were any other than it is, then they would be more contented.*

1. You must know that we are not to choose our own rod, that God shall beat us with.

2. It may be that if it were any other than it is, it would not be so suitable for you as this is. It may be, therefore, God chooses it because it is the most contrary to you, since it is most suitable for purging out the humour that is in you. If a patient comes to take medicine and finds himself sick by it, will he say, 'Oh! if it were any other potion I could bear it?' It may be, if it were any other than it is, it would not suit your disease; yea, if it did not work as it does, it would not suit the disease. So when you say of an affliction, if it were any other than it is, you could bear it, do but answer yourself with this: It may be, if it were any other than it is, it would not be suitable for me. It would not get right to the sinful humour in my soul, and therefore God sees this to be the fittest and the most suitable for me.

3. Know that this is the excellence of grace in a Christian, to be fitted for any condition; not only to say, if it were this or that, but if it were any. Now if a sailor has skill he does not say, 'If it were any other wind but this, if the wind blew in any direction but this, I could manage my ship, I could show skill in other directions but not in this.' Would not sailors laugh at such a one? It would be a shame for him to say that he has skill in any other direction but this. So it should be a shame for a Christian to say that he has skill in any other affliction but this. A Christian should be able to manage his ship, if the wind blows any way; to guide his soul any way.

4. The last answer is this, Know that the Lord has rewards and crowns for all graces, and for honouring them in all conditions. It may be, in such a way as you think you could honour God, God has a crown for that; and God has another crown to set upon the heads of those who honour him in such

a way as this. He has several sorts of crowns, as I may say, in Heaven, and those crowns he must put upon somebody's head, and therefore he exercises you in a variety of conditions, so that you might have the several rewards and crowns that God has to reward and crown those who are faithful in several conditions.

IX. 'Oh, but the condition that God has put me in, makes me unserviceable, and this troubles me. It is true, if it were only an affliction and trouble to myself, it would not be so much, but I am put into such a condition by this affliction that I am unserviceable, and can do God no further service. God has put me into a mean position, and what good can I do? How burdensome is my life to me, because I can do no service for God! That is grievous to me.'

Indeed, if it is true that this is your great grief, it is a good sign. If you can say, as in the presence of God, 'Above all afflictions in this world, I count to be laid aside and not to be employed in the service of God the greatest affliction. I would rather bear any trouble in the world if I might do more service, than be freed from trouble and be laid aside and do little service: can you say so? It is a good sign of grace for a man to account afflictions as great because he can do the Lord but little service. Few men account that an affliction at all.

But yet there may be a temptation in this. To murmur at God's disposal, when your calling is low and mean and you can do little service, is many times a temptation to those who are poor, those who are servants and those who are of weak gifts, and must work hard to provide bread for their families. It is many times a grievous burden to them to think: The Lord uses other men in public service and I live in an obscure way, and to what purpose is my life?

To help against this temptation, that you may not murmur against this condition:

1. Do but consider that though your condition is low and mean, yet you are in the Body, you are a member of the Body, Though you are but a mean member, the toe and the finger have their use in the body; though it is not the eye, though it

is not the head, or the heart, yet it has its use in the body. There is an excellent expression, which I remember Augustine has about this: 'It is better to be the meanest member in the body, than to be the highest and most important member and cut off from the body; it is better to be a little sprig in the tree joined to the root, than to be an arm cut off from the root.' Other men who have but common gifts in the world,* who are not members of Jesus Christ, seem indeed to have more excellence than those who are godly, who are in a mean condition, with mean gifts and mean callings; but they are not of the body, they are not joined to the root, and therefore their condition is worse. When a great arm of a tree is cut off it has a great many leaves on it, and seems a great deal more glorious than those little sprigs that are on the tree, but that little sprig is in a better condition. Why? Because it is joined to the tree and gets sap from the root and flourishes, but the other will wither and die within a while. So it is with all men of the world: they are just like great boughs cut off from the tree; though they have excellent gifts, and have great wealth and pomp and glory in the world, they have no union with Jesus Christ the root. But others who live in a poor condition, a poor tradesman, a poor servant, a poor labouring-man who labours for his family every day, such a one, being godly, may say, 'Though I have but little for the present, little glory, little credit, little comfort, yet I am joined to the Body, and there I have supply and that which will feed me with comfort, blessing and mercy to all eternity.' So all who are in a poor condition in this world, if you are godly, just think of that: though you are mean yet you are in the Body, and joined to the root. You are joined to the principle of comfort, good, blessing and mercy, which will hold out to eternity, when thousand thousands of glorious pompous men in the world shall wither and perish everlastingly. Therefore do not be troubled at your mean condition.

2. Though you have only a mean calling in this world, and so are not regarded as a man of use in the world, yet if you are

* Common gifts as distinct from the gift of salvation.

a Christian, God has called you to a higher calling; your general calling is a high calling, though your particular calling is but low and mean.* There is a place for that in the chapter before my text, Philippians 3. 14: 'I press towards the mark', says the Apostle, 'for the prize of the high calling of God in Christ Jesus.' So every Christian has a high calling of God in Christ Jesus: God has called him to the highest thing to which he has called any creature he has made. The angels in Heaven have not a higher calling than you have. You who perhaps spend your time in a poor business, in the meanest calling, if you are a dung-raker, to rake channels, or to clean places of filth, or any other thing in the world that is the meanest that can be conceived of, your general calling as a Christian advances you higher than any particular calling can advance any man in the world. Others, indeed, who are called to manage the affairs of the State are in a high calling, or ministers, they are in a high calling; but yours in some respects is higher. A poor servant who must be scraping all day about poor, mean things many times may have such a temptation as this: 'Oh, what a poor condition has God put me into! Will God have regard to such a one who is in such a poor, low place as I am?' Oh yes, Christ has regard to the meanest member; as a man has as real a regard to his toe if it is in pain, and will look after it as truly and verily as any other member, so Christ has regard to his lowest and meanest ones.

3. You are in a high calling. Though your outward calling is low in respect of men, yet in respect of God you are in the same calling with the angels in Heaven, and in some degree called to that which is higher, for the Scripture says that the angels come to understand the mystery of the Gospel by the Church. You who are a Christian in that general calling of yours, you are joined with principalities and powers, and with angels, in the greatest work that God has called any creature to, and therefore let that comfort you in this.

4. Your calling is low and mean; yet do not be discontented

* The Puritans taught that believers have a twofold calling: their *particular* calling, which was to their daily occupation and work; and their *general* calling, to be Christians.

with that, for you have a principle within you (if you are a godly man or woman) of grace, which raises your lowest actions to be higher in God's esteem, than all the brave, glorious actions that are done in the world. The principle of faith does it: if any man or woman goes on in obedience to God in a way of faith in the calling in which God has set them – doing this, I say, through a principle of faith – it raises this action, and makes it a more glorious action than all the glorious victories of Alexander and Caesar. All their triumphs and glorious pomp that they had in all their conquests were not so glorious as for you to do the lowest action out of faith. As Luther speaks of a poor milkmaid who is a believer, and does her work in faith: he compares that action to all the glorious actions of Caesar, and makes it a great deal more eminent and glorious in the eyes of God. Therefore faith raises your works which are but mean, and raises them to be very glorious.

Yes, and the truth is, it is more obedience to submit to God in a low calling, than to submit to him in a higher calling; for it is sheer obedience, mere obedience, that makes you go on in a low calling, but there may be much self-love that makes men go on in a higher calling, for there is riches, credit and account in the world, and rewards come in by that, which they do not in the other. To go on quietly in a low calling is more obedience to God.

5. Know further, in the last place, that there is likely to be more reward. For when the Lord comes to reward, he does not examine what work men and women have been exercised in, but what their faithfulness has been. 'Well done, good and faithful servant,' said the Lord; he does not say, 'Well done, good servant, for you have been faithful to me in public works, ruling cities and states, and affairs in kingdoms, and therefore you shall be rewarded.' No, but, 'Well done, good and faithful servant.' Now you may be faithful in little as well as others are in more, by going on and working your day's labour; when you get but a couple of shillings to maintain your family, you may be as faithful in this as those who rule a

kingdom. God looks to a man's faithfulness, and you may have as great a reward for your faithfulness who are a poor servant in the kitchen all the day, as another who sits upon the throne all day. As great a crown of glory you may have at the day of judgment, as a king who sits upon the throne, who has ruled for God upon his throne. Yes, your faithfulness may be rewarded by God with as great glory as a king who has swayed his sceptre for God; because, I say, the Lord does not so much look at the work that is done, as at the faithfulness of our hearts in doing it. Then why should not every one of us go on comfortably and cheerfully in our low condition, for why may not I be faithful as well as another? It is true, I cannot come to be as rich a man and as honourable as others; but I may be as faithful as any other man: every one of you may reason thus with yourselves. What hinders you who are the poorest and meanest from being as faithful as the greatest? Yes, you may have as glorious a crown in Heaven, and therefore go on comfortably and cheerfully in your way.

X. *There is another reasoning that some may have and it is this: 'Oh, I could bear much affliction in some other way, but this is very grievous to me, the unsettledness of my condition.* Even if my condition were low, yet if it were in a settled way, I could be content, but it is so unconstant, and so unsettled, that I never know what to trust to, but am tossed up and down in the world in an unsettled condition, and this is hard to be content with.'

Now to that I answer: 1. The Psalmist says, 'That every man in his settled estate is vanity' (Psalm 39. 5). Your Bibles have it: 'Every man at his best estate is vanity,' the word is, 'his settled estate'. You think, if you were but settled, then you could be content, but the truth is, man in his settled estate is vanity.

2. Perhaps God sees it is better for you to live in a continual dependence upon him, and not to know what your condition shall be on the morrow, than for you to have a more settled condition in terms of the comforts of the creature. Do but remember what we spoke of before, that Christ does not teach

you to pray, 'Lord, give me enough to serve me for two or three years,' but, 'This day our daily bread.' This is to teach us that we must live upon God in a dependent condition every day for daily bread. Here was the difference between the land of Canaan and Egypt: the land of Canaan depended on God for the watering of it with showers from Heaven, but Egypt had a constant way of watering the country, that did not so much depend upon Heaven for water, but upon the river Nile, which at some certain time overflowed the country. Knowing that the watering of their country depended upon the river and not upon Heaven, they grew more proud. And therefore the Scripture, to express Pharaoh's pride, brings him in as saying: 'The river is mine': he could order the river as he pleased, for it was his. Canaan was a country which was to depend upon God, and though they had rain at one time, yet they never knew whether they should have it at another time, and lived always in a dependence upon God, not knowing what should become of them. Now God thought this to be a better land for his people than Egypt, and this is given as one reason among others, that the Lord looked upon it as more suitable to the state of his people, who were to live by faith, that they should be continually depending upon Heaven, upon himself, and not have a constant settled way in the creature for their outward dependence. We find by experience that when those who are godly live in the greatest dependence upon God, and have not a settled income from the creature, they exercise faith more, and are in a better condition for their souls than before. Oh, many times it falls out that the worse your outward estate is the better your soul is, and the better your outward estate is the worse your soul is.

We read in Ezra 4. 13, the objection that the enemies had against the people of Israel's building of the wall of the city: their writing to Artaxerxes against them said, 'Be it known unto the king, that if this city be builded, and the walls set up again, then will not they pay toll, tribute, and custom, and so thou shalt endamage the revenue of the kings.' If the wall be built, they say, then they will refuse to pay toll, tribute and custom to the king, that is, so long as they live in such a condition where they have dependence wholly upon the king, and live at the king's mercy, that is, they are in no city with walls, but the king may come upon them when he will, so long they will pay custom to the king; but if once they come to build a wall, and can defend themselves, and have not their dependence upon the king as before, then they will deny paying toll, tribute and custom. So it is thus, for all the world, between God and men's souls: when a soul lives in mere dependence upon God, so that sensibly he sees that God has advantage of him every moment, Oh, then such a soul will pay toll and custom, that soul exercises faith, and begs every day his daily bread; but if God hedges that man about with wealth, with prosperity – perhaps an inheritance falls to him, perhaps he has a constant office that brings in so much yearly to him duly paid – he is not so sensible now of his dependence upon God, and he begins now to pay less toll and custom to God than before. God has less service from this man now than before. God sees it better for his people to live in a dependent condition. We are very loath in respect of God to be dependent, we would all be independents in this way, we would be dependent upon ourselves and have no dependence upon the Lord, but God sees it better for us to live in a depending condition.

3. This may be your comfort: though for outward things you are mightily unsettled, yet for the great things of your soul and eternal welfare there you are settled. There you have a settled way, a constant way of fetching supply: Of his fulness we receive grace for grace. You have there an abundance of treasure to go to, and get all that you stand in need of. And observe that now your condition is more settled in the Covenant of grace than it was in the Covenant of works: in the Covenant of works God gave man a stock to trade with, but he put it into his hand, so that he might trade, and gain or lose; but in the Covenant of grace, God makes sure: the stock is kept in the hand of Christ, and we must go to him for supply continually, for Christ keeps the stock. Perhaps we may trifle

away something in our trading, but God takes care that we never spend the stock. It is as when a man's son goes bankrupt, having squandered away the capital that he gave him before; afterwards he puts his capital into a friend's hand, and says, 'You shall keep the stock and it shall not be at his disposal.' So we are in a more settled condition in respect of our eternal estate than Adam was in innocence. Therefore let that comfort us in all our unsettled conditions in the matters of the world.

XI. But there is still another reasoning with which many murmuring hearts think to feed their humour. They say, '*If I never had been in a better condition then I could bear this affliction, if God had always kept me in such a low condition, I could be content. Oh, but there was a time when I prospered more, and my hands were full, and therefore now it is harder for me to be brought low, as at present.*' Perhaps a man had five or six hundred a year, but now has had nothing for a great while: if that man had not been born to so much, or had never prospered in any higher degree than he is now in, this affliction would have been less. Perhaps he has some money and friends to live on, but if he had never been in a higher condition, he would not have accounted it so great a thing to have been without it now. This, many times, is our greatest wound, that once we were in a better condition; but it is the most unreasonable thing for us to murmur upon this ground of any.

1. For is your eye evil because God has been good to you heretofore? It is a bad thing for us to have our eye evil because God is good to others, but to look upon our condition with an evil eye now, because God was once good to us! – has God done you any wrong because he was formerly more good to you than he was to others?

2. Did God give you more prosperity before? It was to prepare you for afflictions. We should look at all our outward prosperity as a preparation for afflictions. If you had done so, then it would not have been so difficult for you to endure afflictions now. If when you had great wealth, you made use of

this mercy of God to prepare you for your afflicted estate, then the change of your estate would not be so grievous. Every Christian should say: 'Have I wealth now? I should prepare for poverty. Have I health now? I should prepare for sickness. Have I liberty? Let me prepare myself for imprisonment. How do I know what God may call me to? Have I comfort and peace now in my conscience, does God shine upon me? While I have this let me prepare for God's withdrawing from me. Am I delivered from temptations? Let me prepare now for the time of temptations.' If you would do so, the change of your condition would not be so grievous to you. Sailors who are in a calm prepare for storms; would they say, 'If we never had calms we could bear storms, but we have had calms so many years or weeks together, that this is grievous'? In your calm you are to prepare for storms, and the storm will be less.

You should reason quite contrary to what you do and say: 'Now I am in an afflicted condition, but, blessed be God, I was in a comfortable condition, and, blessed be God, that he was before with me in his mercy': this one consideration may help murmuring hearts. Do you murmur because once you were better? Know that God was before with you in mercy, and you should rather think thus: I have lived for these many years, perhaps forty years or more, in a comfortable condition, I have lived in health, and peace, and plenty; what though the remaining part of my time should have some sorrow and affliction? The Lord has granted to me a comfortable sunshine all the day long towards evening, and what if at seven or eight o'clock at night it begins to rain? Let me thank God I have had such fair weather all day. If you are on a voyage, and you have a comfortable wind, and very fair weather for many months together, what if you have a little storm when you are within sight of land? Will you murmur and repine? Oh no, but you rather bless God that you have had such a comfortable voyage so long. Oh, this consideration would help us all. If God should now say, 'Well, you will never see comfortable days again in outward things in this world', then, you have cause to fall down and bless God's name that you have had so many comfortable days. Now you reason quite contrary: whereas you should bless God that you have had so much comfort, you make what you have had before an aggravation of your afflictions now, and so murmur and are discontented.

On what terms did you hold what God gave you before? Did you hold it so that you have in your papers, 'To have and to hold for ever'? God gives no such thing, God gives to no man, I say, anything but grace to run upon that tenure. There is no such thing in all God's writings for any outward comforts as, 'To have and to hold for you and your heirs.' Indeed, grace he gives to yourselves, to have and to hold for ever, though not for everyone who comes out of your loins to have and to hold for ever; but God does not give any outward thing upon such tenure as that. If God gives me an understanding of himself, and faith, and humility, and love, and patience, and such graces of his Spirit, he gives me them for ever, if he gives me himself, and his Christ, and his promises, and his covenant, he gives me them for ever. Who am I, therefore, that the sun should always shine upon me, that I must have fair weather all my days? What God gives to me, he gave it as a pledge of his love; let me return it to him as a pledge of my obedience. There is all the reason in the world for it: all that a godly man receives from God he receives as a pledge of God's love to him; therefore when he comes into an afflicted condition, God says, 'Return to me as a pledge of your obedience, what you had from me as a pledge of my love.' We should cheerfully come to God and bless God that we have anything to render to him as a pledge of our obedience, and should say, 'Oh, it is your love, O Lord, which has given us everything, which enables us to render a pledge of our obedience to you.' When God calls for your wealth or any comforts that you have, God calls for it as a pledge of your obedience to him.

XII. Another reasoning of a murmuring heart is this: '*Oh, but after I have taken a great deal of pains for this comfort, yet then I am thwarted in it. To be thwarted now after all the labour and pains I have taken, oh, this goes very hard.*'

I answer: 1. The greater the cross, the more obedience and submission.

2. When you took a great deal of pains, was it not with submission to God? Did you take pains, with resolutions that you must have such a thing when you laboured for it? Then know that you did not labour as a Christian, but if you laboured and took pains, was it not with resignation to God?: 'Lord, I am taking pains in my calling, but with submission; I depend wholly upon you for success and a blessing.' And what did you aim at in your labour? Was it not that you might walk with God in the place where God had set you? A Christian should do so in his outward calling: I am diligent in my outward calling, but it is so that I might obey God in it. It is true, I do it that I might provide for my family, but the chief thing that I aim at is that I might yield obedience to God in the way where God has set me. Now if God calls you to another condition, to obey him in, though it is by suffering, you will do it if your heart is right.

3. There will be more testimony of your love to God, if so be that you now yield up yourself to God in what cost you dear. 'Shall I offer that to God', said David, 'that cost me nothing?' Your outward comforts have cost you much, and you have taken great pains to obtain them and now, if you can submit to God in the want of them, in this, I say, your love is the more shown, that you can offer to God what cost you dear.

XIII. Now these are the principal reasonings of a discontented heart. But there is one plea more that may be named: some say, 'Though I confess that my affliction is somewhat hard, and I feel some trouble within me, yet I thank God I do not break out in discontented ways to the dishonour of God; I keep it in, although I have much ado with my own heart.'

Oh, do not satisfy yourselves with that, for the disorders of your hearts, and their sinful workings are as words before God. 'My soul, be silent to God': we spoke of that in the beginning of the expounding of this Scripture. It is not enough for your tongue to be silent; but your soul must be silent. There may be a sullen discontentedness of heart as well as a discontentedness manifested in words, and if you do not mortify that inward sullenness, when you are afflicted a little more, it will break forth at last.

And thus the Lord, I hope, has met with the chief reasonings and pleas for our discontent in our conditions. I beseech you, in the name of God, consider these things, and because they concern your own hearts, you may so much the better remember them. I had thought to have made a little beginning to the next head, which is, Some way of helping you to this grace of contentment. It is a most excellent grace, of admirable use, as you have heard, and the contrary is very sinful and vile.

12

HOW TO ATTAIN CONTENTMENT

Now we are coming to the close of this point of contentment which Jesus Christ teaches those who are in his school. We have opened the point to you, and showed you wherein the art, and skill, and mystery of Christian contentment lies, and many things in the way of application, rebuking the want of it. In the last chapter, I finished that point of showing the various reasonings of a murmuring and discontented heart. I shall now, being desirous to make an end, leave what was said, and proceed to what remains. There are only these two things, for working your hearts to this grace of Christian contentment:

I. To propound several *considerations* for contenting the heart in any afflicted condition.

II. To propound *directions*, what should be done for working our hearts to this.

I. *Considerations to content the heart in any afflicted condition.*

1. We should consider, in all our wants and inclinations to discontent, *the greatness of the mercies that we have, and the meanness of the things that we lack*. The things we lack, if we are godly, are things of very small moment in comparison to the things we have, and the things we have are things of very great moment. For the most part, the things for the want of which people are discontented and murmur are such things as reprobates have, or may have. Why should you be troubled so much for the want of something which a man or woman may have and yet be a reprobate? as, that your

wealth is not so great, your health not so perfect, your credit not so much; you may have all those things and still be a reprobate! Now will you be discontented for what a reprobate may have?

I will give you the example of a couple of godly men, meeting together, Anthony and Didymus: Didymus was blind, and yet a man of very excellent gifts and graces; Anthony asked him if he was not troubled at his want of sight. He confessed he was, 'But', he said, 'should you be troubled at the want of what flies and dogs have, and not rather rejoice and be thankful that you have what angels have?' God has given you those good things that make angels glorious; is not that enough for you, though you lack what a fly has? And so a Christian should reason the case with himself: what am I discontented for? I am discontented for want of what a dog may have, what a devil may have, what a reprobate may have; shall I be discontented for not having that, when God has given me what makes angels glorious? 'Blessed be God,' says the Apostle in Ephesians 1. 3, 'who hath blessed us with all spiritual blessings in heavenly places.' It may be you have not such great blessings in earthly places as some others have, but if the Lord has blessed you in heavenly places, that should content you. There are blessings in heaven, and he has set you here for the present, as it were in heaven, in a heavenly place. The consideration of the greatness of the mercies that we have, and the littleness of the things that God has denied us, is a very powerful consideration to work this grace of contentment.

2. *The consideration that God is beforehand with us with his mercies should content us.* I spoke of this as an aggravation of our discontent, but now I shall use it as a consideration to help us to contentment. You lack many comforts now, but has not God been beforehand with you heretofore? Oh, you have had mercy enough already to make you spend all the strength you have and time you shall live, to bless God for what you have had already. I remember reading of a good man who had lived to fifty years of age and enjoyed his health for eight and

forty years exceedingly well, and lived in prosperity, but the last two years his body was exceedingly diseased, he had the strangury, and was in great pain. But he reasoned the case with himself thus: 'Oh Lord, you might have made all my life a life of torment and pain, but you have let me have eight and forty years in health. I will praise your mercies for what I have had, and will praise your justice for what now I feel.' Oh, it is a good consideration for us, to think that God is beforehand with us, in the way of mercy. Suppose God should now take away your wealth from some of you who have lived comfortably a great while; you will say, 'That aggravates our misery, that we have had wealth.' But it is through your unthankfulness that it does so. We should bless God for what we have had, and not think that we are worse because we have had thus and thus. We might always have been miserable, and, certainly, that man's condition is not very miserable who has no other great aggravation of his misery, but that once he was happy. If there is nothing else to make you miserable, then that is no aggravation that you may not bear, for there is much mercy in that you had it once. Therefore let that content you.

3. *The consideration of the abundance of mercies that God bestows and we enjoy.* It is a saying of Luther: 'The sea of God's mercies should swallow up all our particular afflictions.' Name any affliction that is upon you: there is a sea of mercy to swallow it up. If you pour a pailful of water on the floor of your house, it makes a great show, but if you throw it into the sea, there is no sign of it. So, afflictions considered in themselves, we think are very great, but let them be considered with the sea of God's mercies we enjoy, and then they are not so much, they are nothing in comparison.

4. *Consider the way of God towards all creatures.* God carries on all creatures in a vicissitude of several conditions: thus, we do not always have summer, but winter succeeds summer; we do not always have day, but day and night; we do not always have fair weather, but fair and foul; the vegetative creatures do not always flourish, but the sap is in the root

and they seem to be dead. There is a vicissitude of all things in the world: the sun does not shine always on us here, but darkness comes after light. Now seeing God has so ordered things with all creatures, that there is a mixture of conditions, why should we think it much that there should be a vicissitude of conditions with us, sometimes in a way of prosperity, and sometimes in a way of affliction?

5. The creatures suffer for us; why should not we be willing to suffer, to be serviceable to God? God subjects other creatures, they are fain to lose their lives for us, to lose whatever beauty and excellence they have, to be serviceable to us; why should not we be willing to part with anything in service for God? Certainly, there is not as great a distance between other creatures and mankind, as there is between mankind and God. This is an expression of the martyr, Master Hooper, which we read of in the Book of Martyrs: in labouring to work his own heart, and the hearts of others to contentedness in the midst of his sufferings, he has this comparison, and you may be put in mind of it every day: he said, 'I look upon the creature and see what it suffers to be useful to me. Thus, the brute beasts must die, must be roasted in the fire, and boiled, must come on to the plate, be hacked all in pieces, must be chewed in the mouth, and in the stomach turned to that which is loathsome, if one should behold it; and all to nourish me, to be useful to my body, and shall not I be willing to be made anything for God, for his service? What an abundance of alterations the creature undergoes to be made useful to me, to preserve me! Then, if God will do so with me for his use, as he subjects the creatures to me for my use, why should I not rest contented? If God will take away my wealth, and make me poor, if God will take away life, hack me to pieces, put me in prison – whatever he does, yet I shall not suffer more for God than the creature does for me. And surely I am infinitely more bound to God than the creature is to me, and there is not so much distance between me and the creature, as between me and God!' Such considerations as these wrought the heart of that martyr to contentedness in his sufferings. And every time the creature is upon your plates you may think, What! does God make the creature suffer for my use, not only for my nourishment, but for my delight? what am I, then, in respect of the infinite God?

6. *Consider that we have but a little time in this world.* If you are godly you will never suffer except in this world. Why, do but shut your eyes and soon another life is come, as that martyr said to his fellow martyr, 'Do but shut your eyes', he said, 'and the next time they are opened you shall be in another world.' When he was banished, Athanasius said, 'It is but a little cloud and it will be over, notwithstanding, soon.' These afflictions are but for a moment. When a sailor is at sea he does not think it much if a storm arises, especially if he can see the Heavens clear beyond it; he says, 'It will be over soon.' Consider, we have not long to live, it may be over before our days are at an end. But supposing it should not, death will put an end to all, all afflictions and troubles will soon be at an end by death.

7. *Consider the condition that others have been in, who have been our betters.* We made some use of this before to show the evil of discontent. But, further, it is a mighty argument to work on our hearts a contentedness in any condition. You many times consider who are above you; but consider who are under you.

Jacob, who was the heir both of Abraham and Isaac, for the blessing was on him and the promise ran in him, yet was in a poor, mean condition. Abraham, his grandfather, was able to make a kind of army of his own household, three hundred, to fight with a king, yet Jacob his grandchild goes over Jordan with a staff, and lives in a very poor and mean condition for a long time. Moses might have had all the treasure in Egypt, and some historians say of him, Pharaoh's daughter adopted him for her son, because Pharaoh had no heir for the crown, and so he was likely to have come to the crown. Yet what a low condition he lived in, when he went to live with Jethro his father-in-law forty years on end! Afterwards when he returned to Egypt, with his wife and children, and all that he had, he had only one beast to carry him; he went back to Egypt from his father-in-law in a mean condition.

And we know how Elijah was fed with ravens, and how he had to shift for his life from time to time, and run into the wilderness up and down; and so did Elisha: he was many times in a very low condition; the prophets of God were hid in a cave by Obadiah, and there fed with bread and water; and the prophet Jeremiah put into a dungeon, and oh, how he was used! And it would be endless to name the particulars of the great sufferings of the people of God.

In former time, we have sometimes made use of this argument in other ways: the great instruments of God in the first Reformation lived in great straits, in a very low condition. Even Luther himself, when he was about to die, though he was a man of such public use, and was a great man in the courts of princes, said, 'Lord, I have neither house nor lands, nor estate, to leave anything to wife or children, but I commit them to thee.' And so Musculus who was a very choice instrument of God in his time, though he was a man who was worth even a kingdom for the excellence of his spirit, and learning, for he was one of the most learned men of his time, yet sometimes was forced to dig in the common ditch to get bread for his family. What would we do, if we were in such a condition as these men were?

But, above all, set Christ before us, who professes that the birds of the air had nests, and the foxes had holes, yet the Son of man had no place to hide his head, such a low condition was he in. The consideration of such things as these is very useful. It is likewise useful for men and women of wealth to go to poor people's houses and see how they live, to go to hospitals, and to see the wounds of soldiers and others, and to see the lamentable condition that people live in who live in some alms-houses, and what poor fare they have, and what straits they are put to. You hear sometimes of them, but if you went to see them it would not only stir up charity in yourselves towards them, but stir up thankfulness in your hearts towards God, it would be a special means to help you against any discontent. You would go away and see cause to bless God and say, 'If I were in such a condition as they are in what should I do? How could I bear it? And yet what reason is there that God so orders and disposes of things that they should be so low in their conditions and I so high? I know no reason but free grace: God will have mercy upon whom he will have mercy.' These are good considerations for the furtherance of contentment.

8. *Before your conversion, before God wrought upon your souls, you were contented with the world without grace, though you had no interest in God nor Christ; why cannot you now be contented with grace and spiritual things without the world?* If you yourselves were content with the world without grace, there is reason you should be content with grace without the world. Certainly there is infinitely more reason. You see that many men of the world have a kind of contentment; they do not murmur or repine with the world, though they have no interest in God and Christ. Then cannot you have as much contentment with God and Christ, without the world, as they can, with the world, without God and Christ? It is an infinite shame that this should be so.

9. *Yea, consider, when God has given you such contentments you have not given him the glory.* When God has let you have your heart's desire, what have you done with your heart's desire? You have not been any the better for it; it may be you have been worse many times. Therefore let that satisfy you – I meet with crosses, but when I had contentment and all things coming in, God got but little or no glory from me, and therefore let that be a means now to quiet me in my discontented thoughts.

10. Finally, *consider all the experience that you have had of God's doing good to you in the want of many comforts.* When God crosses you, have you never had experience of abundance of good in afflictions? It is true, when ministers only tell men that God will work good out of their afflictions, they hear them speak, and think they speak like good men, but they feel little or no good; they feel nothing but pain. But

when we cannot only say to you that God has said he will work good out of your afflictions, but we can say to you, that you yourselves have found it so by experience, that God has made former afflictions to be great benefits to you, and that you would not have been without them, or without the good that came by them for a world, such experiences will exceedingly quiet the heart and bring it to contentment. Therefore think thus with yourself: Lord, why may not this affliction work as great a good upon me as afflictions have done before? Perhaps you may find many other considerations, besides, in your own meditations; these are the principal ones that I have thought of.

I will add only one word to this, of one who once was a great merchant and trader – his name was Zeno – and it happened once that he suffered shipwreck, and he said, 'I never made a better voyage and sailed better than at the time that I suffered shipwreck.' Now this was a strange saying that he had never made a better voyage! It would be a strange paradox to you who are seamen, to say that it is a good voyage, when you suffer shipwreck. But he meant because he got so much good by it; God was pleased to bless it so far to him that he gained much to his soul by it, so much soul-riches that he made account that it was the best voyage that ever he had. Truly, sometimes it is so, yes, to you who are godly; I make no question but you find it so, that your worst voyages have proved your best. When you have met with the greatest crosses in a voyage, God has been pleased to turn them to a greater good to you, in some other way. It is true, we may desire crosses that they may be turned to other advantages; but when God in his providence so orders things, that you meet with bad voyages, you may expect that God will turn them to a greater good, and I do not doubt but that those who have been exercised in the ways of godliness any long time, have abundant experiences, which they have gained by them.

You know sometimes it is better to be in a little ship, for they have an advantage over greater ones in storms many times: in a storm a little ship can thrust into a shallow place and so

[214]

be safe, but your great ships cannot, they must be abroad and tossed up and down in the storm and tempest, and so many times split against the rocks. And so, it may be, God sees there is a storm coming, and if you are in your great ship you may be split upon rocks and lands. God, therefore, puts you into a smaller vessel that you may be more safe. We will lay aside speaking of those considerations now, but I would not have you lay them aside, and put them out of your thoughts, but labour (those especially that most concern you) to make use of them in a needful time, when you find any discontentedness of spirit arising in you.

13

HOW TO ATTAIN CONTENTMENT – *concluded*

The main thing that I intend by way of application, is to propound directions, what to do for helping our hearts to contentment. For, as for any further considerations, we have already spoken largely of them, because we have opened most things in showing what the lessons are that Christ teaches men, when he brings them into his school, to teach them this art. I say, we have spoken there of the special things that are most considerable for helping us to this grace of contentment. Therefore, now, all that I shall further do about this point, will be the giving of some directions, what course to take that we may come to attain this grace of contentment.

1. *All the rules and helps in the world will do us little good unless we get a good temper within our hearts.* You can never make a ship go steady, by propping it outside; you know there must be ballast within the ship, to make it go steady. And so, there is nothing outside us that can keep our hearts in a steady, constant way, but what is within us: grace is within the soul, and it will do this.

2. *If you would get a contented life, do not grasp too much of the world, do not take in more of the business of the world than God calls you to.* Do not be greedy of taking in a great deal of the world, for if a man goes among thorns, when he may take a simpler way, he has no reason to complain that he is pricked with them. You go among thorns – is it your way? Must you of necessity go among them? Then it is another matter. But if you voluntarily choose that way, when you

may go another, then you have no cause to complain. If men and women will thrust themselves on things of the world which they do not need, then no wonder that they are pricked, and meet with what disturbs them. For such is the nature of all things here in this world, that everything has some prick or other in it. We will meet with disappointments and discontentments in everything we meddle with, and therefore those who have least to do in the world, that is, unless God calls them to it (we must put in that), are likely to meet with many things that will dissatisfy them.

3. *Be sure of your call to every business you go about.* Though it is the least business, be sure of your call to it; then, whatever you meet with, you may quiet your heart with this: I know I am where God would have me. Nothing in the world will quiet the heart so much as this: when I meet with any cross, I know I am where God would have me, in my place and calling; I am about the work that God has set me. Oh, this will quiet and content you when you meet with trouble. What God calls a man to, in that he may have comfort whatever befalls him. God will look to you, and see you blessed if you are in the work God calls you to.

4. What has just been said is especially true if I add: *That I walk by rule in the work that I am called to.* I am called to such a business, but I must manage this work that I am called to by rule. I must walk by the Word, order myself in this business according to God's mind as far as I am able. Now add this to the other, and then the quiet and peace of the soul may be made even perfect in a way. When I know that I have not put myself on the work, but God has called me to it, and I walk by the rule of the Word in it, then, whatever may come, God will take care of me there. It was a saying of a heathen: 'If you will subject all things to yourself, subject yourself to reason and by that you will make all things to be under you.' I may add a little more to it: if you will subject all things under you, subject yourself to God, and then, the truth is, all things are under you.

It has been as many times we have hinted: the reason why

many of our gentry have been so malignant among us is, because they are willing to be slaves themselves under some above them at Court, so that they may keep their neighbours under, to be slaves to them, for, you know, any man before who was great at Court, could crush any countryman with whom he was angry. If there were an arbitrary government, then all those who would be willing to be vassals and slaves to the Prince could make all others vassals and slaves under them. Now be willing to be a vassal to God, to be absolutely under God's command, and then, I say, all things in the world are under you. 'All things are yours,' says the Apostle, 'life and death, every thing is yours, and you are Christ's, and Christ is God's.' All things in the world are serviceable to that man or woman who is serviceable to God. It is a mighty commendation of God's service: be willing to be serviceable to God yourself and God makes all things in the world your servants, for so they are. You will say, 'How are they my servants? I cannot command them.' They are servants in this, that God orders them all to work for your good. There is nothing in the world but, says God, it shall work for your good, and be serviceable to you, if you will be serviceable to me.' Who would not be now God's servant? Subject yourself to God, and all things shall be subjected to you.

So long as we keep within our bounds, we are under protection, but if once we break our bounds, we must expect it to be with us as it is with the deer in the park: while the deer keep within the pale, no dogs come after them, and they can feed quietly, but let the deer get outside the pale, and then every dog in the country will be hunting after them. So it is with men: let men and women keep within the bounds of the command of God, of the rule that God has set them in his Word, and then they are protected by God, and they may go about their business in peace, and never be troubled for anything, but cast all their care upon God. God provides for them. But if they go beyond the pale, if they pass their bounds, then they may expect to meet with troubles, and afflictions, and discontent. And therefore that is a fourth direction: walk by rule.

5. *Exercise much faith;* that is the way for contentedness. After you have done with all the considerations that reason may suggest to you, if you find that these do not do it, Oh, then, call for the grace of faith. A man may go very far with the use of reason alone to help him to contentment, but when reason is at a nonplus, then set faith at work. It was a saying of the reverend divine, Master Perkins, whom God made so useful in his time: 'The life of faith', he said, 'is a true life, indeed the only life.' Exercise faith, not only in the promise that all shall work together for good to them that fear God, but likewise exercise faith in God himself; as well as in his Word, in the attributes of God. It was a saying of Socrates, a heathen: 'Since God is so careful for you, what need you be careful for any thing yourselves?' – it was a strange saying for a heathen.

Oh, Christian, if you have any faith, in the time of extremity think thus: this is the time that God calls for the exercise of faith. What can you do with your faith, if you cannot quiet your heart in discontent. There was a saying of one Dionysius, who had been a king, and afterwards was brought to such a low condition as to get his living by being a schoolmaster: someone comes and asks him, 'What have you got by your philosophy from Plato and others?' 'What have I got,' he says, 'I have got this, that though my condition is changed from so high a condition to low, yet I can be content.' So what do you get by being a believer, a Christian? What can you do by your faith? I can do this: I can in all states cast my care upon God, cast my burden upon God, I can commit my way to God in peace: faith can do this. Therefore, when reason can go no higher, let faith get on the shoulders of reason and say, 'I see land though reason cannot see it, I see good that will come out of all this evil.'

Exercise faith by often resigning yourself to God, by giving yourself up to God and his ways. The more you in a believing way surrender up yourself to God, the more quiet and peace you will have.

6. *Labour to be spiritually minded.* That is, be often in

meditation of the things that are above. 'If we be risen with Christ,' say the Scriptures, 'let us seek the things that are above, where Christ is, that sits at the right hand of God.' Be much in spiritual thoughts, in conversing with things above. Many Christians who have an interest in the things of Heaven converse but very little with them; their meditations are not much upon heavenly things. Some give this as the reason why Adam did not see his nakedness, they think that he had so much converse with God and with things above sense, that he did not so much mind or think of what nakedness was. Whether that were so or not I will not say, but this I say, and am certain of, the reason why we are so troubled with our nakedness, with any wants that we have, is because we converse so little with God, so little with spiritual things; conversing with spiritual things would lift us above the things of the world. Those who are bitten or struck by a snake, it is because they tread on the ground; if they could be lifted up above the earth they need never fear being stung by the snakes which are crawling underneath. So I may compare the sinful distemper of murmuring, and the temptations and evils that come from that, to snakes that crawl up and down below; but if we could get higher we should not be stung by them. A heavenly conversation is the way to contentment.

7. *Do not promise yourselves too much beforehand; do not reckon on too great things.* It is good for us to take hold very low, and not think to pitch too high. Do not soar too high in your thoughts beforehand, to think, Oh, if I had this and this, and imagine great matters to yourselves; but be as good Jacob: you know he was a man who lived a very contented life in a mean condition, and he said, 'Lord, if I may but have clothes to put on, and meat to eat.' He looked no higher, he was content with that. So if we would not pitch our thoughts high, and think that we might have what others have, so much and so much, we would not be troubled so much when we meet with disappointments. So Paul says, 'If we have but meat and drink and clothing, let us be therewith content.' He did not soar too high aloft. Those who look at high things in the world meet

with disappointments, and so they come to be discontented. Be as high as you will in spiritual meditations; God gives liberty there to any one of you to be as high as you will, above angels. But, for your outward estate, God would not have you aim at high things; 'Seekest thou great things?' said the Lord to Baruch, 'seek them not' (Jeremiah 45. 5), you shall have your life for a prey. In these times especially, it would be a very great evil for anyone to aim at great things; seek them not, be willing to take hold low, and to creep low, and if God raises you, you will have cause to bless him, but if you should not be raised, there would not be much trouble. One who creeps low cannot fall far, but it is those who are on high whose fall bruises them most. That is a good rule: do not promise yourselves great things, neither aim at any great things in the world.

8. *Labour to get your hearts mortified to the world, dead to the world.* We must not content ourselves that we have gotten some reasoning about the vanity of the creature, and such things as these, but we must exercise mortification, and be crucified to the world. Paul said, 'I die daily', we should die daily to the world. We are baptized into the death of Christ, that is to signify that we have taken such a profession as to profess to be even as dead men to the world. Now no crosses that fall out in the world trouble those who are dead; if our hearts were dead to the world we should not be much troubled with the changes of the world, nor the tossings about of worldly things. It is very noteworthy in those soldiers who came to break the bones of Christ, that they broke the legs of one who was crucified with him, and of the other, but when they came to Christ, they found he was dead, and so they did not break his legs; there was a providence in it, to fulfil a prophecy, but because they found he was dead, they did not break his bones. Let afflictions and troubles find you with a mortified heart to the world, and they will not break your bones; those whose bones are broken by crosses and afflictions are those who are alive to the world, who are not dead to the world. But no afflictions or troubles will break the bones of

one who has a mortified heart and is dead to the world; that is, they will not be very grievous or painful to such a one as is mortified to the world. This, I fear, is a mystery and riddle to many, for one to be dead to the world, to be mortified to the world. Now it is not my work to open to you what mortification is, or death to the world is, but only what it is to have our hearts so taken off from the things of the world, as that we use them as if we used them not, not accounting that our lives, our comforts, our happiness consist in these things. The things in which our happiness consists are of a different kind, and we may be happy without these: this is a kind of deadness to the world.

9. *Let not men and women pore too much upon their afflictions:* that is, busy their thoughts too much to look down into their afflictions. You find many people, all of whose thoughts are taken up about what their crosses and afflictions are, they are altogether thinking and speaking of them. It is just with them as with a child who has a sore: his finger is always on the sore; so men's and women's thoughts are always on their afflictions. When they awake in the night their thoughts are on their afflictions, and when they converse with others—it may be even when they are praying to God – they are thinking of their afflictions. Oh, no marvel that you live a discontented life, if your thoughts are always poring over such things. You should rather labour to have your thoughts on those things that may comfort you. There are many who, if you propound any rule to them to do them good, will take it well while they are with you, and thank you for it, but when they are gone they soon forget it. It is very noteworthy of Jacob, that when his wife died in child-birth, she called the child Ben-oni, that is, a son of sorrows; but Jacob thought with himself, If I should call this child Ben-oni, every time that I name him it will put me in mind of the death of my dear wife, and of that affliction, and that will be a continued affliction to me, therefore I will not have my child have that name, and so the text says that Jacob called his name Benjamin, the son of my right hand. Now this is to show us thus much, that when

[222]

afflictions befall us we should not give way to having our thoughts continually upon them, but rather upon those things that may stir up our thankfulness to God for mercies.

There is a comparison made by Basil, a learned man: It is in this case as with men and women who have sore eyes: now it is not good for them to be always looking into the fire, or at the beams of the sun. 'No', he says, 'one who has sore eyes must get things that are suitable to him, and such objects as are fit for one with such weak eyes.' Therefore they get green colours, as being a more easy colour and better for weak eyes, and they hang green sarsenet before their eyes because it is more suitable to them. It is the very same with weak spirits. A man or woman who has a weak spirit must not be looking into the fire of their afflictions, upon those things that deject, that cast them down, but they ought to be looking rather on that which may be suitable for healing and helping them; they should consider those things rather than the other. It will be of very great use and benefit to you, if you lay it to heart, not to be poring always on afflictions, but on mercies.

10. I beseech you to observe this, though you should forget many of the others: *Make a good interpretation of God's ways towards you*. If any good interpretation can be made of God's ways towards you, make it. You think it much if you have a friend who always makes bad interpretations of your ways towards him; you would take that badly. If you should converse with people with whom you cannot speak a word, but they are ready to make a bad interpretation of it, and to take it in an ill sense, you would think their company very tedious to you. It is very tedious to the Spirit of God when we make such bad interpretations of his ways towards us. When God deals with us otherwise than we would have him do, if one sense worse than another can be put upon it, we will be sure to do it. Thus, when an affliction befalls you, many good senses may be made of God's works towards you. You should think thus: it may be, God intends only to try me by this, it may be, God saw my heart was too much set on the creature, and so he intends to show me what is in my heart, it may be, that

[223]

God saw that if my wealth did continue, I should fall into sin, that the better my position were the worse my soul would be, it may be, God intended only to exercise some grace, it may be, God intends to prepare me for some great work which he has for me: thus you should reason.

But we, on the contrary, make bad interpretations of God's thus dealing with us, and say, God does not mean this; surely, the Lord means by this to manifest his wrath and displeasure against me, and this is but a furtherance of further evils that he intends towards me! Just as they did in the wilderness: 'God hath brought us hither to slay us.' This is the worst interpretation that you can possibly make of God's ways; oh, why will you make these worst interpretations, when there may be better? In 1 Corinthians 13. 5, when the Scripture speaks of love, it says, 'Love thinketh no evil.' Love is of that nature that if ten interpretations may be made of a thing, nine of them bad and one good, love will take that which is good and leave the other nine. And so, though ten interpretations might be presented to you concerning God's ways towards you, and if but one is good and nine bad, you should take that one which is good, and leave the other nine.

I beseech you to consider that God does not deal by you as you deal with him. Should God make the worst interpretation of all your ways towards him, as you do of his towards you, it would be very ill with you. God is pleased to manifest his love thus to us, to make the best interpretations of what we do, and therefore God puts a sense upon the actions of his people that one would think could hardly be. For example, God is pleased to call those perfect who have any uprightness of heart in them, he accounteth them perfect: 'Be ye perfect as your heavenly Father is perfect'; uprightness in God's sense is perfection. Now, alas, when we look into our own hearts we can scarce see any good at all there, and yet God is pleased to make such an interpretation as to say, It is perfect. When we look into our own hearts, we can see nothing but uncleanness; God calls you his saints, he calls the meanest Christian who has the least grace under the greatest corruption his saint.

You say we cannot be saints here, but yet in God's esteem we are saints. You know the usual title the Holy Ghost gives, in several of the Epistles, to those who had any grace, any uprightness, is, to the *saints* in such a place; you see what an interpretation God puts upon them, they are saints to him. And so I might name in many other particulars, how God makes the best interpretation of things; if there is an abundance of evil and a little good, God rather passes by the evil and takes notice of the good.

I have sometimes made use of a very notable place in Peter, concerning Sarah: Sarah had a speech to her husband in Genesis 18. 12, she called her husband *lord*. There was only that one good word in a bad, unbelieving speech; but yet when the Apostle mentions that speech in 1 Peter 3. 6, the Holy Ghost leaves all the bad, and commends her for calling her husband 'lord', for putting a reverent title upon her husband. Thus how graciously God deals with us! If there is but one good word among a great many ill, what an interpretation God makes! So should we do, if there is only one good interpretation that we can make of a thing we should rather make use of the good one than the bad. Oh, my brethren (I would I could now speak only to such as are godly), retain good thoughts of God, take heed of judging God to be a hard master, make good interpretations of his ways, and that is a special means to help you to contentment in all one's course.

11. *Do not so much regard the fancies of other men, as what indeed you feel yourselves.* For the reason of our discontentment many times is rather from the fancies of other men than from what we find we lack ourselves. We think poverty to be such a great evil – Why? because it is so esteemed by others, rather then that people feel it so themselves, unless they are in an extremity of poverty. I will give you a clear demonstration that almost all the discontent in the world is rather from the fancies of others than from the evil that is on themselves. You may think your wealth to be small and you are thereupon discontented, and it is a grievous affliction to you; but if all men in the world were poorer than you, then you

would not be discontented, then you would rejoice in your estates though you had not a penny more than you have. Take a man who can get but his twelve pence a day, and you will say, This is but a poor thing to maintain a family. But suppose there were no man in the world that had more than this, yea, that all other men but yourselves had somewhat less wages than you, then you would think your condition pretty good. You would have no more then than you have now; therefore it appears by this that it is rather from the fancies of other men than what you feel that makes you think your condition to be so grievous, for if all the men in the world looked upon you as happy, more happy than themselves, then you would be contented. Oh, do not let your happiness depend upon the fancies of other men. There is a saying of Chrysostom I remember in this very case: 'Let us not make the people in this case to be our lords; as we must not make men to be the lords of our faith, so not the lords of our comforts.' That is, our comfort should not depend more upon their imaginations, than upon what we feel in ourselves. It may be, others think you to be in an afflicted condition, yea, but I thank God, for myself I do not so apprehend it. Were it not for the disgrace, disregard and slightings of other men, my condition would not be so bad to me as it is now. This is what makes my condition afflictive.

12. *Be not inordinately taken up with the comforts of this world when you have them*. When you have them, do not take too much satisfaction in them. It is a certain rule: however inordinate any man or woman is in sorrow when a comfort is taken from them, so were they immoderate in their rejoicing in the comfort when they had it. For instance, God takes away a child and you are inordinately sorrowful, beyond what God allows in a natural or Christian way; now though I never knew before how your heart was towards the child, yet when I see this, though you are a mere stranger to me, I may without breach of charity conclude that your heart was immoderately set upon your child or husband, or upon any other comfort that I see you grieving for when God has taken it away. If you hear ill tidings about your estates, and your hearts are

dejected immoderately, and you are in a discontented mood because of such and such a cross, certainly your hearts were immoderately set upon the world. So, likewise, for your reputation, if you hear others report this or that ill of you, and your hearts are dejected because you think you suffer in your name, your hearts were inordinately set upon your name and reputation. Now, therefore, the way for you not to be immoderate in your sorrow for afflictions is not to be immoderate in your love and delights when you have prosperity.

These are the principal directions for our help, that we may live quiet and contented lives.

My brethren, to conclude this point, if I were to tell you that I could show you a way never to be in want of anything, I do no doubt but then we should have much flocking to such a sermon, when a man should undertake to manifest to people how they should never be in want any more. But what I have been preaching to you now comes to as much. It countervails this, and is in effect all one. Is it not almost all one, never to be in want, or never to be without contentment? That man or woman who is never without a contented spirit, truly can never be said to want much. Oh, the Word holds forth a way full of comfort and peace to the people of God even in this world. You may live happy lives in the midst of all the storms and tempests in the world. There is an ark that you may come into, and no men in the world may live such comfortable, cheerful and contented lives as the saints of God. Oh, that we had learned this lesson.

I have spent many sermons over this lesson of contentment, but I am afraid that you will be longer in learning it than I have been preaching of it; it is a harder thing to learn it than it is to preach or speak of it. I remember I have read of one man reading of that place in the 39th Psalm, 'I will take heed that I offend not with my tongue'; he said, I have been these thirty-eight years learning this lesson and have not learned it thoroughly. The truth is, there are many, I am afraid, who have been professors near eight and thirty years, who have hardly learned this lesson. It would be a good lesson, for young professors to begin to learn this early. But this lesson of Christian contentment is as hard, and perhaps you may be many years learning it. I am afraid there are some Christians who have not yet learned not to offend grossly with their tongues. The Scripture says that all a man's religion is vain if he cannot bridle his tongue; therefore one would think that those who make any profession of godliness should quickly learn this lesson, such a lesson that, unless learned, makes all their religion vain. But this lesson of Christian contentment may take more time to learn, and there are many who are learning it all the days of their lives and yet are not proficient. But God forbid that it should be said of any of us concerning this lesson, as the Apostle says of widows, in Timothy, That they were ever learning and never came to the knowledge of the truth. Oh let us not be ever learning this lesson of contentment and yet not come to have skill in it. You would think it much if you had been at sea twenty years, and yet had attained to no skill in your art of navigation; you will say, I have used the sea twenty or thirty years and I hope I may know by this time what concerns the sea. Oh, that you would but say so in respect of the art of Christianity! When anything is spoken concerning the duty of a Christian, Oh, that Christians could but say, I have been a Christian so long, and I hope I am not wanting in a thing that is so necessary for a Christian. Here is a necessary lesson for a Christian, that Paul said, he had learned in all estates therewith to be content. Oh, do not be content with yourselves till you have learned this lesson of Christian contentment, and have obtained some better skill in it than heretofore.

Now there is in the text another lesson, which is a hard lesson: 'I have learned to abound.' That does not so nearly concern us at this time, because the times are afflictive times, and there is now, more than ordinarily, an uncertainty in all things in the world. In such times as these are, there are few who have such an abundance that they need to be much taught in that lesson.